MW00949293

Information Technology
in a
Global Society

for the IB Diploma

Solutions Book

Stuart Gray

Information Technology in a Global Society — Solutions Book

Unless otherwise noted, all material is © Copyright 2011-2013 Stuart Gray. All rights reserved. No part of this work covered by the copyright herein may be reproduced or transmitted in any form or by any means, electronic, mechanical, photocopying, recording, or otherwise, without prior written permission of the author.

Product names, logos, brands, and other trademarks featured or referred to within this text are the property of their respective trademark holders.

This textbook has been developed independently of the International Baccalaureate®.

Information Technology in a Global Society

for the IB Diploma

Solutions Book

Stuart Gray

Using this textbook

Information Technology in a Global Society is the first textbook written specifically for the new IB Information Technology in a Global Society syllabus, covering technical systems, social impacts and ethical issues, and each area of application. The book has a number of features to enhance teaching and understanding and ensure students get the best experience possible from the ITGS course.

Solutions Book

This solutions book has assessment rubrics and possible answers for all of the written exercises in the textbook—over 200 in total. To make using this book easier, the following layout has been used:

Assessment rubrics are located at the back of the book. These are clearly referenced from the individual questions that use them. Each rubric is on a separate page to allow for easier photocopying, and has ample space for writing student feedback on copies.

Extended response essay questions include thorough lists of possible answers. To maintain consistency, these essay questions should be graded according to the IB® ITGS extended response rubric for SL and HL paper 1. This can be found online in the ITGS specimen papers (occ.ibo.org).

Students may take different approaches in answering questions. While the answers in this text provide thorough list of possible answers, it is highly likely that students may think of other feasible answers. Students should not be penalised for writing correct answers that are not mentioned in the solutions here.

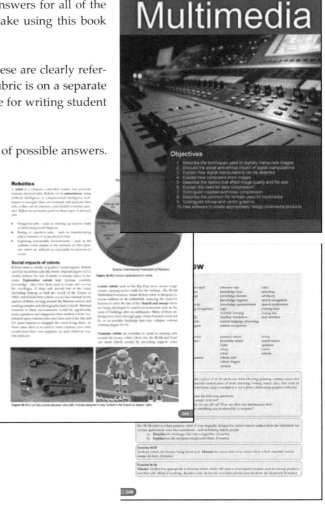

Chapter 6

Online Support and Resources

This textbook's website (www.itgstextbook.com) provides additional resources to support the use of the book. Students can find useful links to examples and case studies related to the topics covered in the text, while teachers can find additional activities, exercises and exam questions, and rubrics for the main exercises.

In addition, the ITGS News blog (www.itgsnews.com) provides regular posts with news articles, lesson ideas, and resources related to ITGS and technology teaching in general.

Contents

Introduction

Credits

Chapter 1
Introduction

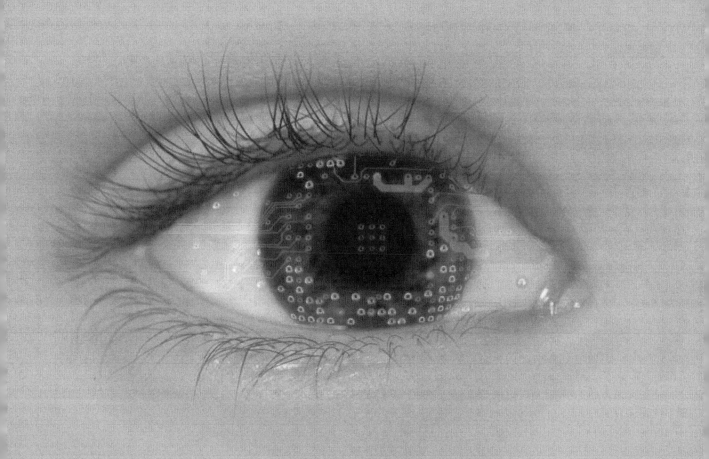

Chapter 1 Solutions

Exercise 1-1
1) G
2) J
3) F
4) C
5) B
6) D
7) A
8) E
9) H
10) I

Exercise 1-2
Students should find articles which clearly exhibit:

- Information being input (possibly automatically)
- Processing of information
- Output of information
- Storage and communication of information may also be present.

Processing of information is the key stage. If data is merely input and then stored or output without processing (for example, a surveillance camera which records to hard disk), it is not an example of information technology in the context of ITGS.

Exercise 1-3
Students can use the textbook support site, www.itgstextbook.com to find a list of popular RSS readers. They can also download a bundle of common RSS feeds to import into their readers.

Exercise 1.4
Grade according to the rubric on page 120.

Exercise 1.5
Grade according to the rubric on page 121.

Exercise 1-6
a) ITGS related. There is clear input (the soldiers' inputs into the game), processing of information (calculation of movements, enemy positions, bullet trajectories), and output (graphical and sound output to depict the results of these interactions). ITGS issues raised might include People and Machines (the realism of the methods soldiers use to interact with the game) and the Reliability and Integrity of the game (its accuracy compared to real life).

b) ITGS related. There is input (the setup of the world and the children's inputs), processing of information (calculation of movements and interaction in the virtual world), and output (the results of their interaction). ITGS issues might include Globalisation (the world provides students with an opportunity to access a wealth of data not normally available to them) and Digital Citizenship (regarding correct online behaviour and online safety).

c) Not ITGS related. Although television companies make extensive use of computers in the production of their shows, there is no information processing involved in watching them. (If the topic were violent video games, the processing would arise from the interaction of the players, which would be an ITGS topic).

d) ITGS related. The Internet (including the World Wide Web) satisfies the criteria for an information system, and the possible social impacts of excessive use are clearly ITGS issues.

e) ITGS related, but does not raise any significant social or ethical issues. Although music players satisfy the criteria for an information system, there are no significant issues raised by the release of one model. Often students who write about topics such as this make huge generalizations or vague assumptions (for example "people will be happier because they can listen to their music anywhere"), which does not fit into the ITGS requirement for thorough analysis and evaluation.

Exercise 1-7
a) The use of software-controlled medical devices.

Possible answers include:
Positive impacts
- Health impacts—improved accuracy compared to human surgeons may allow previously impossible surgery (for example targeting a tumour growing extremely close to organs).
- Health impacts—Smaller incisions reduce patient pain and scarring, and improve recovery time.
- Monitoring can be performed constantly without the need for medical personal (thus fewer staff are required / more patients can be treated).
- Staff can be alerted automatically if a vital sign reaches a certain threshold (e.g. heart rate drops below a certain value).

- Remote monitoring of patients (i.e. in their own homes) may be possible—increasing patient independence. Similarly, remote surgery is possible with some equipment.

Negative impacts
- Reliability of software and hardware may be a concern which could have negative health impacts on the patient if a failure occurs.
- The cost of such devices may be prohibitive for some hospitals and patients, preventing access.
- Psychological—Patients may fear (rightly or wrongly) the use of such technology during their operation.

b) The creation of digital copies of famous works of art

Possible answers include:
Positive impacts
- Artwork may be made available to a wider audience (for example on art gallery or museum web sites).
- High quality copies can be made and displayed, while the original is stored for protection.
- Art restorers can test out various restoration methods without damaging the original.
- Digital copies can be incorporated into other works (promotional material, t-shirts, mugs) which can be sold for a profit.

Negative impacts
- The value of the original may be reduced by the availability of cheap copies (intellectual property issues).
- The original may be damaged during the process of creating the image (for example, dropping the work, tearing the work, or even light from scanners fading the work).
- Digital copies will never be 100% accurate copies of the original – they are limited by scanning resolution, for example.

c) The increased use of mobile phones by young people, especially school children

Possible answers include:
Positive impacts
- Parents can maintain contact with their children, knowing their whereabouts and improving safety.
- Mobile Internet capabilities can give access to a wealth of free information whenever needed (such as in the classroom).

Negative impacts
- Parents can find it harder to control the content children access on (Internet equipped) phones—children have easy access to a wide range of undesirable material.
- Excessive use can disrupt a child's routine – for example, late night calls and messages disturbing sleep
- Expensive mobile phones may make a child a target for theft or assault.
- The negative health impacts of extensive mobile phone use have not yet been conclusively disproven.

d) The use of the Internet to cast votes in national elections

Possible answers include:
Positive impacts
- Young people may be encouraged to vote as they tend to be more engaged with technology.
- People unable to travel to a voting both (busy at work, no transport) may vote.
- People with disabilities may find it more accessible to vote online.
- All voters may find online voting beneficial in terms of transport costs (for example, fuel) and time spent travelling and waiting in line.

Negative impacts
- Preventing unauthorised access to the cast votes is a significant challenge (Security issue).
- Votes may be accidentally changed or ignored due to faulty hardware or software (Reliability and Integrity issue).
- Some security and authentication techniques may store user details, which violates the right to secret ballots (Privacy issue).
- It can be difficult to authenticate a user's identity over the Internet.
- It is more difficult to prevent voter intimidation when they vote from their own homes.
- Paper voting still needs to be available, otherwise those without computers or the skills to use them become disenfranchised (Equality of access issue).

Exercise 1-8
Possible answers include:

Factors affecting a search engine's ranking
- Number of links to a page from other sites (more is better).
- 'Quality' of the sites linking to a page (higher is better).
- Payment by page owner (though sponsored links usually appear in a separate section of the results pages).
- Amount of duplicate / unique content on a page (duplicate content is penalised).
- How recently the page was updated (more recent content is often prioritised, especially in certain categories such as news reports).
- Certain pages may be excluded from the results due to legal requirements (for example, sites which illegally house copyrighted material).
- Certain key words may be blocked or heavily filtered due to legal requirements (for example, terms related to religious and political freedom in China).
- User preferences may prioritise certain results (such as those in a specified language).
- User browsing history may be used to prioritise certain results based on sites frequently visited ('personalised search results').
- Certain sites may be prioritised based on recommendations ('Likes') from users on social networks ('social search').

This may affect our knowledge by:
- Presenting us with the "popular view" of a topic even if it is not necessarily accurate (witness how Wikipedia frequently appears at the top of certain types of searches).
- Limiting our view by only showing us a small subset of pages (how many users go beyond the first page, or even half page, of search results?).
- Preventing us from viewing certain pages altogether (if a search engine blocks the page).
- Presenting us with pages similar to those we already view (based on our history), thus limiting our exposure to alternative viewpoints and reinforcing our existing ones.
- Failing to notify us that results are filtered, so we are unaware that alternative viewpoints exist.

Chapter 2
Hardware

Chapter 2 Solutions

Exercise 2-1

Possible answers include:

- Batteries with longer lives—these have enabled more power-hungry features such as colour screens and cameras with video functionality.
- Smaller batteries—these have enabled smaller, more portable devices.
- Developments in flash memory (solid state storage) with greater storage capacities—these have enabled greater functionality (such as video recording and document / file storage).
- Touch screen technology—this has reduced the need for a keyboard, enabling smaller phones.
- Faster and lower power processors—these have enabled more complex software, including games and web browsers with multimedia features.
- Developments in wireless communication (3G and 4G) have allowed greater bandwidth—these have enabled faster Internet access / multimedia browsing.
- Higher resolution screens—these have enabled games, video, and photo viewing features.

Award 1 mark for identifying the development and 1 mark for describing how it has contributed to smart phones, up to a maximum of 3 answers.

Exercise 2-2

Students should compare computers based on the specifications listed in the book. Ensure the correct units are used:

- Processor speed (in MHz or GHz)
- RAM (in MB, GB, or TB)
- Hard disk capacity (in MB, GB or TB)

Exercise 2-3

Possible answers include:

- Ability to take photographs (previously required a separate camera).
- Ability to record videos (previously required a separate video camera).
- Ability to record audio (previously required a separate tape recorder or similar device).
- Ability to play music (previously required a portable music player or similar device).
- Ability to listen to the radio on the move.
- Ability to watch television on the move.
- Ability to play games (previously required a (portable) games console).
- Ability to browse the Internet (previously required a separate computer / laptop).
- Ability to store documents / data (previously required a portable secondary storage device such as a flash drive).
- GPS functionality (previously required separate GPS receiver).

Grade according to the 4 mark Explanation rubric on page 140.

Exercise 2-4

Possible answers include:

Manufacturers

- Create these devices and choose to use harmful chemicals—indicating they have at least some responsibility.
- Profit from the sale of these devices so should pay for their clean-up—indicating they have at least some responsibility.
- Create the problem by continually releasing new products (driving the upgrade-cycle)—indicating they have at least some responsibility.
- Could benefit by accepting back their own products and reusing the components or materials.
- Could use their equipment take-back schemes to promote a "green image" for their business.

Customers

- Benefit from these devices, so have responsibility for their safe disposal.
- Have safe disposal options available to them—but may need educating about their availability.
- Could "vote with their wallet" by only buying from manufacturers with environmentally-friendly policies.
- Are the driving force for upgrades and new models.

Other stakeholders

- Governments have a responsibility to provide / regulate safe recycling facilities.
- Governments have a responsibility to prevent e-waste exports (in MEDCs) and e-waste imports (in LEDCs).
- Can enforce safe recycling or the use of less harmful chemicals by making it a legal requirement.

This exercise should be marked according to the generic ITGS extended response rubric for SL and HL Paper 1. This can be found in the ITGS Specimen Papers.

Exercise 2-5
Possible answers include:
Benefits

- Students are often familiar with these devices which may improve participation in PE lessons.
- Students may be encouraged to participate in real versions of the sports they play on the console.
- Logging features can record students' fitness levels over time, so they can see clear progress.
- This may be one of the few ways to encourage some students to participate in physical activity.
- There may be less embarrassment for some students (for example, doing poorly at a sport in front of the whole class, or being a weak member of a team).
- These games may be more accessible to students with certain disabilities.
- Some schools may lack sports facilities such as playing fields, making consoles a viable alternative.

Problems

- Gaming equipment can be expensive to purchase—making it hard to outfit an entire class.
- Gaming equipment needs to be secured against theft and protected from damage.
- These games do not teach the same skills as actual sports—for example, teamwork and strategy, team spirit, coordination, or the same type of physical fitness.

This exercise should be marked according to the ITGS generic mark band for SL and HL Paper 1 Part (c). This can be found online in the ITGS Specimen Papers.

Exercise 2-6
Possible answers include:
a) An ATM
Input devices:

- Magnetic stripe reader *(do not allow "credit card reader" or "card reader")*
- Keypad to input PIN
- Buttons to make menu selections
- Touch screen

Output devices:

- Money output slot
- Printer (for receipts)
- Speaker / beeper
- Screen

Storage devices:

- Hard disk

b) An airport self check-in machine
Input devices:

- Keyboard to input flight details
- Software keyboard / virtual keyboard to input flight details
- Buttons to make menu selections
- Touch screen
- Optical reader / scanner (for passport details)
- RFID reader (for passport details)

Output devices:

- Screen
- Speaker
- Printer for boarding pass

Storage devices:

- Hard disk

c) A mobile phone (cell phone)

Input devices:

- Keyboard
- Software keyboard / virtual keyboard
- Touch screen
- Microphone
- Buttons

Output devices:

- Speaker
- Screen

Storage devices:

- Solid state storage / flash memory / memory card

d) An in-car GPS navigation system

Input devices:

- Buttons
- Keyboard
- Software keyboard / virtual keyboard
- Touch screen

Output devices:

- Screen
- Speaker

Storage devices:

- Solid state storage / flash memory / memory card

e) An aircraft cockpit

Input devices:

- Joystick
- Pedals
- Buttons
- Levers
- Switches
- Keyboard

Output devices:

- Speakers
- Screens
- Lights
- Motors / hydraulic output (movement of aircraft)

Storage devices:

- Solid state storage / flash memory
- Magnetic tape (in Flight Data Recorder ("black box") devices)

f) A cleaning robot

Input devices:

- Ultra-sonic sensor
- Light sensor
- Infra-red sensor
- Touch sensor
- Vibration sensor
- Buttons (to control / setup robot)

Do not allow 'sensor' without a specified type

Output devices:

- Wheels
- Motor
- Lights
- Speaker

Storage devices:

- Solid state storage / flash memory

Exercise 2-7

Grade according to the rubric on page 122.

"Average" specifications change over time, so the figures here should be taken as guidelines. More important is the relative difference between the computers chosen – the solution for scenario B, for example, should have a significantly higher specification than that for scenario A.

Students should not be awarded marks if they have chosen computers which are excessively over-specified, since this does not meet the definition of "suitable".

Suitable specifications include:

Scenario A:

- An averagely specified computer is suitable here .
- There is no need for a particularly fast processor, large amounts of RAM or a high capacity hard disk.
- A laptop or desktop might be chosen.
- A printer could be a useful peripheral device.
- A scanner could be a useful peripheral device.

Scenario B:

- Ample hard disk space is required – in the region of 1 TB upwards—for storing video.

- A large, high resolution screen is useful for running video editing software.

- Large amounts of RAM (4 GB upwards) is important for loading many large video clips at once.

- A fast processor (or a dual or quad-core processor) is important for rendering video effects.

- A desktop computer rather than a laptop would be the best choice as they typically have higher specifications.

Scenario C:

- A laptop / netbook should be chosen (not a desktop computer) for portability.

- A smaller laptop would be most suitable.

- A larger laptop could be justified (for example, a larger screen reduces eye strain, or larger keyboard makes document creation easier).

- A lightweight laptop would be good.

- Battery life should be referenced in relation to the question (i.e. 2.5 hours or more)

- A fast processor is not required as the tasks being performed are basic.

- Large amounts of RAM are not required.

- Large amounts of secondary storage (hard disk or flash memory) are not required.

- A hard disk is suitable but flash storage could be justified in terms of reliability (linked to possible hard disk damage during travel).

Exercise 2.8

Note: Several newer versions of the OLPC with updated specifications have been developed or proposed. However, as of December 2012 none of these have been released.

Possible answers include:

- 433 MHz CPU—low power and requires no cooling fans, prolonging battery life.

- Flash memory secondary storage—offers improved reliability compared to hard disks (no moving parts).

- Wireless 'mesh' network—allows networking without the need for additional equipment (e.g. router).

- Hardened, dust and water proof case—designed specifically for use by young children in harsh environments.

- LED LCD screen—which is low cost, easy to replace, and reduces power consumption.

- Optional equipment includes solar panel charger and hand crank charger—designed for use in areas where electricity may be scarce or expensive.

- Lack of removable media (floppy disk and CD/DVD drive) - a choice made to reduce power consumption.

This exercise should be marked according to the generic ITGS extended response rubric for SL and HL Paper 1. This can be found in the ITGS Specimen Papers.

Exercise 2-9

(a)

(i) Megahertz (MHz) or Gigahertz (GHz)

(ii) Gigabytes (GB) or Terabytes (TB)

(b)

Possible answers include:

- eSATA connection

- USB connection

- FireWire connection

(c)

- Primary storage is volatile (loses its contents when the power is removed) whereas secondary storage is non-volatile / permanent.

- Primary storage is used to store programs and data currently being used, while secondary storage is used to store all programs and data, even if not in use.

- Primary storage is much faster to access (as it is electronic) than secondary storage (which is mechanical)

- Primary storage exists in smaller quantities (typically a few gigabytes at most) whereas secondary storage exists in very large quantities (typically several terabytes)

Award 1 mark per item plus 1 mark for the contrasting statement, up to a maximum of 4 marks.

(d)

A standard CD-R holds either 650 MB or 700 MB.

1 MB = either 1024 KB or 1000 KB

Accept either 1000 or 1024 in the following calculation:

    1500 KB / 1000 = 1.5 MB

    700 MB / 1.5 MB = 466.67

    =466 photographs

Alternatively, convert the CD size to kilobytes first:

    700 MB × 1000 = 700,000 KB

    700,000 KB / 1500 KB = 466.67

    = 466 photographs

Award 1 mark for the correct answer and 1 mark for the correct working / calculations.

Exercise 2-10

(a)

A computer which is found inside another device (such as a washing machine or a car's engine) *[1 mark]*, and performs a single specialised function *[1 mark]*.

(b)

Possible answers include:

- Microphone and voice recognition software
- Microphone and text-to-speech software
- Trackball
- Eye-tracking software
- Head wand
- Input switches
- Sip and puff input device
- Braille keyboard

(c)

- Supercomputers are typically designed for extremely high speed complex calculations.
- Mainframes are typically designed for very high data throughput with less complex calculations.

Award 1 mark if the student only identifies the properties / features of one side (i.e. the supercomputer or the mainframe). Award 2 marks if the student covers both sides correctly.

(d)

Possible answers include:

i) Touch screen

- User interfaces on mobile phones or tablet computers
- User interfaces on public kiosks (for example, airport check in or photo booth kiosks)

ii) OMR

- Reading multiple choice exam answers (e.g. SAT). *(Do not allow answers that do not indicate multiple choice)*
- Reading multiple choice survey answers *(Do not allow answers that do not indicate multiple choice)*
- Reading the number choices on lottery tickets

Barcode readers

- Scanning items at a shop checkout / Point of Sale
- Checking items entering / leaving facilities such as warehouses
- Identifying and routing baggage in airports

Track ball

- Small portable devices such as mobile phones or some laptops
- Situations where theft of a mouse is a risk (for example, in public kiosks or terminals)
- Situations where desk space is at a premium (for example, some industrial computers)
- They can be used by disabled users who might find them easier to use than a mouse.

Chapter 3
Software

Chapter 3 - Software

Exercise 3-1

Grade according to the rubric on page 123.

Notes: In this exercise it is a good idea to look for common mistakes including large generalisations made without supporting evidence (for example "commercial software is more secure", "commercial software is easier to use" - or vice versa).

Exercise 3-2

Grade according to the rubric on page 124.

This exercise could also be completed as a written assignment using the same or a similar rubric.

Exercise 3-3

1) F
2) I
3) E
4) H
5) B
6) A
7) C
8) K
9) D
10) L
11) G
12) J

Exercise 3-4

Grade according to the rubric on page 125.

Exercise 3-5

In this exercise students should consider:

- The fact that no system is 100% reliable.
- The types of places safety critical systems are found.
- The types of impact caused by the failure of a safety critical system.
- That safety critical software clearly needs a lower rate of failure than other software.
- That fall-back or redundant mechanisms can reduce the impact of a safety critical system failure.

- That there are 'sensible' ways and 'dangerous' ways for a system to fail (for example, traffic lights should all fail to red, not to green).
- The essential nature of many safety critical systems and the lack of feasible alternatives.

Grade according to the 4 mark Explanation rubric on page 140.

Suggesting "no failures" is the only acceptable rate should be considered a significant error as it suggests the student has not understood that all computer systems will fail at some point.

Exercise 3-6

a)
(i) 1 Gigabyte (GB)
(ii) 40 Gigabytes (GB)

The units must be specified.

b)
Possible answers include:
An operating system is software which:

- Manages the computer's hardware
- Manages a system's resources
- Assigns resources to programs
- Manages running programs
- Manages system security (for example file access or system login)

Award 1 mark for "software" plus 1 mark for one of the task descriptions.

c)
Possible answers include:
Arguments in favour of its suitability

- The system includes office application software and anti-spyware / anti-virus tools: these are essential items for IB students.
- The specification of the machine is sufficient for most common student tasks: word processing, using spreadsheet and presentation software, and Internet browsing.
- The computer includes all required peripheral devices including keyboard and screen.
- The low specification of the machine means the price is likely to be low.

Arguments against its suitability

- The processor is relatively slow—how much of a disadvantage this is depends on the software used (and IB courses taken).

- The amount of RAM is low: this limits certain uses such as graphics or video editing, which the student may need depending on his IB courses.

- The hard disk capacity is low: this may cause problems for some students (e.g. IB Film students wishing to save lots of video).

- The supplied operating system is old: this may cause problems as modern application software may require a newer OS.

- The supplied operating system is old: it may no longer be supported by the developer in terms of help and (security) updates.

- The supplied office software is Open Office: documents may not be compatible with some application software used at the school.

- Upgrading the system may be hard due to its age and the lack of available parts.

This exercise should be marked according to the generic ITGS extended response rubric for SL and HL Paper 1. This can be found in the ITGS Specimen Papers.

Chapter 4
Networks

Chapter 4 Solutions

Exercise 4-1

Grade according to the 4 mark Explanation rubric on page 140.

Acceptable answers vary depending on the school's network. Most school networks are likely to be client-server configurations.

Sample answer:

The school network is a client-server network. There are many examples of clients: Windows desktop computers in the computer labs, Mac desktop computers in the library, and laptops used by various teachers around the school. Student owned computers are also client computers.

Files and programs are stored on the school's central server so they are accessible regardless of which client computer a person uses. Each client must login to the school network before the files and programs can be accessed. The server also shares some devices (such as printers) so they are accessible by all users.

Exercise 4-2

Ensure the devices are connected in the correct sequence:
- *Servers should be connected to hubs, routers, or switches*
- *Clients should be connected to hubs, routers, or switches*
- *Clients should **not** be directly connected to servers*
- *Shared devices can be connected directly to hubs, routers, switches, clients, or servers, depending on the network configuration.*

See sample diagram below.

Sample diagram for Exercise 4-2

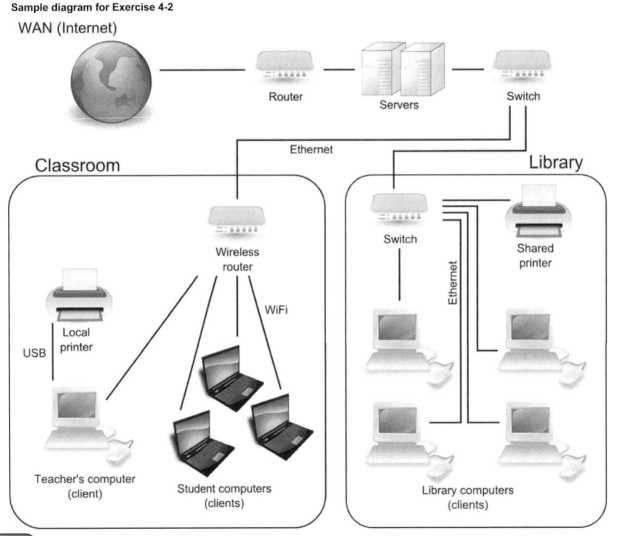

Exercise 4-3

Possible answers include:

- Total Cost of Ownership: Thin clients can have lower specifications (and therefore be cheaper) than fat clients because most work is performed by the server.
- Total Cost of Ownership: older computers can be utilised instead of discarded, since all processing is done on a separate server.
- Total Cost of Ownership: Low specification thin clients consume less power and thus reduce running costs.
- Management: Thin clients allow more centralised software management by delivering it from the server over the network. There is no need to install or maintain software on every individual machine.
- Reliability: data is centralised on servers, making backup processes easier.
- Security: Thin clients without secondary storage devices make it harder to introduce malware (either deliberately or accidentally).
- Security: Data theft from individual clients is reduced because no data is stored locally.
- Intellectual property: Thin clients without secondary storage devices make it harder to introduce unauthorised or unlicensed software (for which the company may be legally responsible).
- Better use can be made of available storage capacity (i.e. there is no need for every client to have a hard disk, each of which may only be 50% full)

Grade according to the 6 mark Explanation rubric on page 141.

Exercise 4-4

1) C
2) A
3) B
4) E
5) D
6) F
7) G
8) L
9) K
10) H
11) I
12) J

Exercise 4-5

For these questions it is essential that students remember network speeds are measured in bits per second, not bytes per second.

a) A 400 Kilobyte image over a dial up connection

56 Kilobits per second is typical maximum speed for a MODEM.

> 56 Kbps / 8 = 7 Kilobytes per second
> 400 KB / 7 KB = 57.14 seconds

Award 1 mark for the correct answer and 1 mark for the correct working / calculations.

b) A 300 MB software download on a 1MB cable connection

Accept 1000 or 1024 in the following calculation:

> 1 Mbps = 1000 Kbps
> 1000 Kbps / 8 = 125 Kilobytes per second
> 300 MB × 1000 = 300,000 KB
> 300,000 / 125 = 2,400 seconds
> = 40 minutes

Award 1 mark for the correct answer and 1 mark for the correct working / calculations.

Exercise 4-6

215 Kilobytes × 8 = 1,720 kilobits

A 2 megabit connection is an acceptable answer since ISPs typically sell 'round number' speeds.

Award 1 mark for the correct answer and 1 mark for the correct working / calculations.

Exercise 4-7

Possible answers include:

Hardware:

- A router to connect the home network to the Internet (probably supplied by the ISP).
- The above router should have Wi-Fi capabilities OR a separate wireless router can be purchased, to connect the laptops to the Internet.
- Ethernet cables may be needed for the desktop computer OR a wireless network card can be purchased for this computer.

Software:

- The parents might consider network monitoring or filtering software depending on the age of their children, to provide increased online safety.
- Anti-virus, anti-spyware, or anti-malware software should be considered to provide increased security.
- Firewall software might be considered for individual machines to protect against unauthorised network access.

Award 1 mark for the correct answer and 1 mark for the explanation, up to 4 marks.

Exercise 4-8

Possible answers include:

Provision: Restriction on the installation of unauthorised software.
Reason: To prevent possible infection by malware, and issues related to unlicensed copies of software.

Provision: No unauthorised access / hacking into other systems.
Reason: The company might be held legally responsible for actions performed using its networks and systems.

Provision: Restriction on access to social media sites
Reasons: Staff can waste time on such sites, reducing productivity. Company image can also be harmed by "unauthorised" social media posts. Bandwidth can be wasted on such sites.

Provision: Restriction on access to inappropriate sites including adult-content, obscene, offensive, or illegal material.
Reasons: Adult / obscene content can offend fellow workers, creating an uncomfortable working environment. The company might be held legally responsible for illegal content downloaded using its networks and systems.

Provision: No sharing passwords / accounts with other users. Users are responsible for all activity performed using their account.
Reason: Security can easily be breached in this way. Audit logs are less useful if multiple people share a single account.

Provision: No disclosure of confidential company information online.
Reasons: The company may be held legally accountable for breaches of data protection laws. The loss of confidential information can have a negative impact on the company / benefit competitors.

Provision: No posting of abusive or derogatory comments targeting about users, companies, or organisations.
Reason: The company might be held legally responsible for actions performed using its networks and systems (including cases of employee harassment).

Award 1 mark for the provision and 1 mark for the explanation, up to 4 answers.

Exercise 4-9

a)

Network neutrality:

- A concept in which all web site traffic is treated equally (no prioritisation of certain traffic).
- This affects stakeholders by ensuring all web sites are on a "level playing field" and can compete equally.

Two-tier Internet

- A 'two-tier Internet' would allow companies to pay money to have Internet Service Providers prioritise their traffic and send it before unpaid traffic.
- This affects stakeholders by allowing richer companies to pay for their web sites to load faster than companies who cannot afford to pay (potentially damaging competition).

Award 1 mark for the outline and 1 mark for the effect on the stakeholder, up to 4 marks.

b)

Grade according to the 4 mark Explanation rubric on page 140.

Sample answer:

Deep packet inspection would need to occur: this involves checking each packet of data sent over the network for its content, source, and destination. This could occur at the Internet Service Provider. These details could be checked against a database of companies who have paid for priority service: if present in the database, data could be routed immediately. If not present, data could be routed only after all paid traffic has been routed.

c)

Possible answers include:

Benefits of network neutrality

- The system is fundamentally equal, treating everybody the same regardless of the money they have available.
- This enables small businesses to easily compete online with larger business on an equal footing.

Drawbacks of network neutrality

- All traffic is treated equally, which means heavy users can congest the network for others.

Benefits of a two-tier Internet

- A two-tier system will generate revenue that can be ploughed back into infrastructure.

Drawbacks of a two-tier Internet

- Costs may increase for businesses, which may be passed on to customers.
- Economic growth could be harmed as smaller businesses struggle to compete with richer ones.
- Users may be charged a premium for high speed access to certain sites (for example, video streaming sites).
- Privacy may be invaded (network monitoring is needed to effectively shape traffic).

This exercise should be marked according to the ITGS generic mark band for SL and HL Paper 1 Part (c). This can be found online in the ITGS Specimen Papers.

Exercise 4-10

a)

Possible answers include:

- Hub
- Switch
- Router
- Client
- Server

b)

A type of network configuration in which client computers possess minimal processing and storage capabilities *[1 mark]*, and processing is performed by a remote server over the network. *[1 mark]*

c)

Possible answers include:

- Share settings can be used to allow access to specific users or groups of users.
- File system permissions can be used to allow access to specific users or groups of users.
- Access can be granted / blocked to specific IP addresses.
- Access to specific services running on specific ports (for example, port 80, http) can be granted / denied.

Grade according to the 6 mark Explanation rubric on page 141.

Exercise 4-10 (question 4-10 repeated by mistake)

(a)

- Bits per second (bps)
- Kilobits per second (Kbps)
- Megabits per second (Mbps)
- Gigabits per second (Gbps)

Do not allow answers involving bytes per second.

b)

A network of computers spread over a large area *[1 mark]* such as a city or a large university campus. *[1 mark]*

c)

Possible answers include:

- Each network device has a unique hardware address, known as the MAC address, embedded in it.
- On a TCP/IP network, each machine on a local area network is assigned a private IP (Internet Protocol) address, which uniquely identifies that machine on the network.
- On the Internet, each 'Internet-facing' computer is also assigned an IP address. Private IP addresses within the local network are not visible to other computers on the Internet. Web sites typically use domain names (such as www.itgstextbook.com) to identify them. DNS servers are used to associate a given domain name with the IP address of the web server holding the site.

Grade according to the 6 mark Explanation rubric on page 141.

Exercise 4-11

a) False

b) False (private IP addresses can be duplicated on separate LANs)

c) False

d) True

e) False

f) True

g) False

h) True

i) True

Chapter 5
Security

Chapter 5 Solutions

Exercise 5-1

Students should consider the passwords they use in their everyday lives. In general, answering "no" to two or more of the columns, having a short password, or having a password that has not been recently changed would be considered poor practice.

Exercise 5-2

Possible answers include:

Hand biometric

a)
- Width of palm
- Height of palm (wrist to finger base)
- Pattern of lines on palm
- Length of (a specified) finger
- Width of (a specified) finger
- Vein patterns
- Palm print (the area touching the sensor)

b)
- High resolution images of the palm need to be obtained.
- Short term damage to the hand could cause reader problems.

c)
- Over time the biometric might change somewhat (for example, skin changes as a person ages).

d)
- Individual measurements may be very similar in two or more individuals.
- A combination of several measurements is less likely to be the same in two individuals.
- Research has shown vein patterns to be unique to individuals.

e)
- General purpose, non-invasive authentication systems to provide access to secure areas (e.g. on doors).
- There have been experiments with palm print recognition in firearms to prevent illegal use or accidental use by children.

Fingerprint biometric

a)
- Pattern of ridges and lines on the fingerprint
- Width of the fingerprint
- Height of the fingerprint

b)
- Short term injuries to the finger (for example, cuts) can cause issues with the biometric recognition.

c)
- Several systems have proven to be vulnerable to fake fingerprints.

d)
- Fingerprints are unique, even in identical twins. However, biometric systems do not consider the entire fingerprint, but a number of points on it.

e)
Fingerprints are widely used, including:
- Access to laptop computers
- Access to secure areas
- School registration / meal payment / library systems for students
- Some cars use thumb prints to recognise the driver and adjust the seats and mirrors to their preference.

Do not allow: "crime scenes" or similar, since these are not uses of fingerprint biometrics for authentication purposes.

Body biometric

a)
- Height (head to toe)
- Shoulder width
- Waist width
- Inside leg length
- Head width
- Gait (walking style)

b)
- Capturing a biometric sample can be difficult
- The sample process is made more difficult by certain types of clothes or headwear that can obscure measurements.
- The technology can cause privacy concerns as biometric samples can be captured without the subject's knowledge.
- Walking style can vary depending on walking surface, shoes worn, or terrain type.

c)
- Many of these aspects of a person's physique can change over time (for example, as they age or as weight is gained or lost).

d)
- Height and width measurements in particular can be similar to other people.
- Even a combination of the two is not guaranteed to generate unique results.

e)
- Can be used in applications where a passive scan (possibly without the subject's knowledge) is required.
- Identification based on gait (full body biometric combined with an individual's walking style) has been used in British courts.
- Can be used or applied "after the fact" - for example, by using these techniques to analyse CCTV video footage, even if the system was not originally set up for this purpose.

Exercise 5-3
a)
Possible answers include:
- The system does not disrupt the flow of fans in the stadium—this makes it a better choice for use with large numbers of people, with minimum inconvenience.
- Biometric samples can be taken from subjects without their knowledge (i.e. they may not be aware that they are being photographed) - this is a privacy concern.
- The technique can be applied anywhere a video camera exists. This means it can be used in a huge number of places, very cheaply.

Grade according to the 4 mark Explanation rubric on page 140.

b)
- A false negative occurs when the system fails to identify a known criminal. This could allow them stadium access without the additional security measures that might otherwise be applied.
- A false positive occurs when the system incorrectly identifies an innocent (unknown) person as a known criminal. This could cause inconvenience to the person as they may be stopped, subject to additional security, or even detained.

Award 1 mark for the correct description of a false positive / false negative, and 1 mark for the expansion, up to 4 marks.

c)
Possible answers include:
Benefits
- Large numbers of people can be scanned with relative ease.
- The system may deter troublemakers from attending the game, reducing potential problems and crime for everyone.
- The system can be applied throughout the stadium—not just at the gates, but using CCTV cameras in grandstands and other areas.
- The system can be applied "after the fact" - for example, if an incident becomes known after the game, the system can be applied to recorded CCTV footage.

Drawbacks
- Biometric samples are taken from all fans—even innocent people. This raises privacy concerns over how the data is used and how long it is kept.
- Inaccuracies in the system (false positives) could cause great inconvenience for innocent people.
- The system may give a false sense of security—people may forget that it cannot detect criminals or troublemakers who are not known to the police.

This exercise should be marked according to the generic ITGS extended response rubric for SL and HL Paper 1. This can be found in the ITGS Specimen Papers.

Exercise 5-4
a)
Assuming 26 lower case letters only

$$26^{10} = 141,167,095,653,376 \text{ combinations}$$
$$141,167,095,653,376 / 10,000,000$$
$$= 14,116,709.57 \text{ seconds}$$
$$= 163 \text{ days (worst case scenario)}$$

b)
26 lowercase letters plus 26 uppercase letters = 52 letters

$$52^{10} = 144,555,105,949,057,024 \text{ combinations}$$
$$144,555,105,949,057,024 / 10,000,000$$
$$= 14,455,510,594.91 \text{ seconds}$$
$$= 458 \text{ years (worst case scenario)}$$

c)
26 lowercase letters, 26 uppercase letters, 10 digits, assume 25 symbols = 87 characters

87^{15} combinations

123,819,426,824,732,821,912,024,192,743 / 10,000,000 =

12,381,942,682,473,282,191,202.42 seconds

= 392,628,826,816,123.86 years (worst case scenario)

Exercise 5-5

Students should investigate web browser features including:

- Anti-phishing filters
- Blocking of known malware downloads
- Blocking of known phishing / malware web sites
- Virus-scanning of downloaded files
- Blocking of cross-site "click-jacking"
- Automatic updates to patch security holes
- Automatic updates to known phishing / malware site lists identified above

Example answer:

Phishing sites are a risk as they imitate genuine organisations such as banks and attempt to trick users into handing over sensitive details such as credit card numbers, usernames, and passwords. Clearly this has a potential to cause a serious economic impact on the user through fraud. Several organisations maintain lists of known phishing sites and update them frequently. Browsers such as Mozilla Firefox use these lists to automatically block known sites, displaying a clear warning message when the user tries to visit them. This only works for known phishing sites, so users should still be cautious.

Grade according to the 4 mark Explanation rubric on page 140.

Exercise 5-6

Describe computer crime laws

A good way to complete this task is for students to research laws in their own country. After considering these laws, students should become aware (perhaps through comparing their work) how much cybercrime laws vary internationally.

Well known computer security related laws include:

- *Computer Misuse Act*
- *CAN-SPAM Act*
- *Computer Fraud and Abuse Act*
- *Electronic Communications Privacy Act*
- *Identity Theft Enforcement and Restitution Act*

Award 1 mark for identifying the law and 1 mark for the correct description of the provisions it provides.

Why disparate global laws might cause problems

Possible answers include:

- Acts illegal in one country may be legal in another.
- Determining legal jurisdiction is difficult: laws may apply from the webmaster's country of residence, the country hosting the content, or the content in which the content is accessed.
- Some countries may have weak law enforcement, making prosecution difficult.
- Affecting arrests and/or legal action is difficult because of these points.

Grade according to the 4 mark Explanation rubric on page 140.

Exercise 5-7

- When connecting to a secure website the browser setups up a TLS or SSL connection.
- The user enters their credit card details (plaintext).
- These are encrypted with the site's public key to produce the ciphertext.
- The ciphertext is transmitted over the Internet to the recipient.
- The ciphertext is decrypted by the recipient using their private key.

Award 1 mark per step up to 4 marks.

Exercise 5-8

Possible answers include:

Benefits

- The volume of spam sent could be reduced.
- A side effect could be the reduction in fake email accounts (since email accounts must be tied to a credit card with a real name to allow payment).

Drawbacks

- The infrastructure and setup costs could be enormous; these might be passed on to users.
- Users would effectively need a credit card in order to use email, cutting off many users (for example those without credit cards, children).
- Security and fraud concerns could arise from the vast increase in online credit card use.
- Privacy concerns could arise since personal details (including physical addresses) must be given to email providers.
- This could be seen as a way of punishing genuine users for the crimes of a few rogue users.
- A lot of spam is sent via botnets of hijacked computers, so these measures might not help.

This exercise should be marked according to the generic ITGS extended response rubric for SL and HL Paper 1. This can be found in the ITGS Specimen Papers.

Exercise 5-9
Grade according to the rubric on page 126.

Exercise 5-10
Laws requiring handover of encryption keys
- Only suspects are required to compromise their security by handing over encryption keys or passwords (compared to other methods).
- Some encryption software (e.g. TrueCrypt) offers 'plausible deniability' features so it is unclear if a system still contains further encrypted data.
- Some criminals may prefer a jail sentence for refusing to reveal encryption keys than the longer sentence they may receive if their data is decrypted.

Key escrow schemes
- Escrow organisations have a great responsibility to keep the keys they hold secure—unauthorised access to the keys could impact thousands of users.
- Only legitimate users are likely to provide their encryption keys for escrow—criminals are likely to ignore such requirements.

Limiting the strength of available encryption
- Free and open source encryption software offering extremely strong encryption is already widely available on the Internet—this would be hard to stop.
- Weaker encryption exposes businesses and organisations to attacks from skilled cyber-criminals, putting their business secrets and data at risk.

This exercise should be marked according to the generic ITGS extended response rubric for SL and HL Paper 1. This can be found in the ITGS Specimen Papers.

Exercise 5-11
This survey is designed to test students' understanding of security measures and to find out more about people's general understanding of security. A common mistake is for students to make this survey a test—for example "What is a computer virus?". Instead they should focus on assessing understanding of security measures—for example "Do you have anti-virus software installed?".
The data from this task can be used in a practical spreadsheet exercise.

Exercise 5-12
a) WPA (Wireless Protected Access) is a form of encryption *[1 mark]* used to protect data travelling over wireless networks from unauthorised access. *[1 mark]*

b)
Spam refers to unsolicited email which is usually sent in bulk. *[1 mark]* Often spam features advertisements for illicit products or schemes. *[1 mark]*

Phishing is a form of spam (it is also unsolicited email). *[1 mark]* The key difference is that phishing emails impersonate an existing organisation or company using fake logos, web sites, email addresses and other material to trick the user into revealing sensitive details such as passwords. *[1 mark]*

c) *Assuming Bob is sending a message to Alice:*
- Bob creates his message (the plaintext)
- Bob obtains Alice's public key (which should be publicly available)
- Bob encrypts the plaintext into ciphertext using Alice's public key
- The ciphertext is transmitted to Alice
- Alice decrypts the ciphertext using her private key to reveal the plaintext.

Award 1 mark per step up to 4 marks.

Exercise 5-13
a)
Identity theft is a criminal act involving using personal data about a person to impersonate them. *[1 mark]* This is usually done to gain services, money, or products.
[1 mark]

b) Pharming is the process of illicitly changing DNS records of web sites. *[1 mark]* This means that when a user enters the domain name of a website, they are transferred to false or fake web site (usually used for phishing).
[1 mark]

c)
Possible answers include:
Measure: Encrypt the hard disk
Explanation: This makes the data inaccessible without a password or security token. This ensures the data on the disk cannot be read by an unauthorised user should the laptop be lost or stolen. This is particularly important for laptop owners because such devices are more easily lost / stolen.

Measure: Use strong passwords on user accounts
Explanation: In the event that the laptop is lost or stolen, a password will prevent a casual user from accessing the data on the device. A strong password (using mixed case letters, numbers, and symbols) is important to ensure that the password cannot be easily guessed or found using password cracking tools.

Measure: Wireless connections should be secured
Explanation: The user should only connect to wireless networks that use WPA or WPA2 encryption. This protects data travelling over the network from unauthorised eavesdroppers. Users should avoid WEP encryption as it is an old standard and easily cracked.

Award 1 mark for identifying the advantage and 1 mark for the explanation, up to 6 marks.

Do not allow "Make a backup copy" as this does not protect the data on the device itself.

Exercise 5-14
a)
Possible answers include:
- A mix of uppercase and lowercase letters should be used
- A mix of numbers and letters should be used
- A mix of symbols and letters should be used
- The password should not be a name or a word found in a dictionary
- The password should not be a simple modification of a real word (for example, password123)
- The password should be of sufficient length – minimum 10 characters, preferably longer
- The password should be changed often
- The password should be unique—i.e. the same password should not used for multiple accounts

b)
Possible answers include:
Method: Performing a dictionary attack
Explanation: This involves using software to automatically try all words in a dictionary one by one until the correct password is found.

Method: Performing a brute force attack
Explanation: This involves using software to try all combinations of letters, numbers, and symbols one by one until the correct password is found.

Method: Social engineering
Explanation: This involves tricking the user into revealing their password, perhaps by looking over their shoulder as they type it is, or sending a phishing email.

Method: Using a key logger
Explanation: An attacker may use a software or hardware key logger to record all the user's keystrokes, thus revealing their password.

Award 1 mark for identifying the advantage and 1 mark for the explanation, up to 4 marks.

c)
Possible answers include:
Advantage: Biometric details cannot be forgotten
Explanation: Biometric features such as fingerprints, iris scans, or voice prints cannot be forgotten or lost, unlike a traditional password or security token. This makes them more convenient in some situations.

Advantage: Reduced risk of theft or loss
Explanation: Because they are cannot be written down and are not typed into a computer, they cannot be stolen by spyware and are much less susceptible to physical theft.

Disadvantage: Biometric features are irrevocable and cannot be changed
Explanation: In the event that biometric data is somehow reproduced (for this possibility, see page 293 of the textbook), the system is completely compromised: unlike a password, an iris scan or fingerprint cannot easily be changed.

Disadvantage: Privacy and security concerns may be raised
Explanation: The collection of biometric data may raise privacy concerns, particularly if the subject is a child. Users may be concerned about how their biometric data will be stored and who it will be shared with. This is also important from a security point of view.

Award 1 mark for identifying the advantage and 1 mark for the explanation, up to 2 marks. Award 1 mark for identifying the disadvantage and 1 mark for the explanation, up to 2 marks.

Exercise 5-15

a)

Possible answers include:

- Fingerprints
- Palm (vein) recognition
- Iris scan
- Voice recognition
- Handwriting recognition
- Typing style recognition

b)

A false positive is when a system gives a positive result when it should not (for example, incorrectly saying two fingerprints match when they do not).

A false negative is when a system gives a negative result when it should not (for example, incorrectly saying two fingerprints do not match when in fact they do).

Award 1 mark for the basic description and 1 mark for the expansion, up to 4 marks.

c)

Enrolment stage:

- Each user's identity is established (for example using identification documents) and they are asked to provide a biometric sample (for example, a fingerprint)
- A mathematical biometric template is produced from this sample
- The biometric template is stored along with the user's credentials (such as their name)

During use:

- A user provides a biometric sample (for example, a fingerprint)
- A biometric template is produced from this sample
- This biometric template is compared with the biometric template stored on the system during the enrolment stage
- If there is sufficient similarity between the two templates, the user is granted access; otherwise access is denied

Award 1 mark per step up to 4 marks.

Exercise 5-16

a) SSL (Secure Socket Layer) is a protocol used on the world wide web to encrypt web pages [1 mark] to prevent them being viewed by unauthorised users as they are transmitted across a network. *[1 mark]*

b)

Possible answers include:

Method: Padlock icon in the address bar or browser status bar. (*Do not allow "on the web page"*)
Description: Indicates a secure connection (using SSL or TLS encryption) is established, preventing unauthorised access to data being sent and received.

Method: Https instead of http in the address bar
Description: Indicates a secure connection (using SSL or TLS encryption) is established, preventing unauthorised access to data being sent and received.

Method: Address bar changes colour (e.g. yellow or green)
Description: Indicates a secure connection (using SSL or TLS encryption) is established, preventing unauthorised access to data being sent and received.

Method: Organisation's name appears in the address bar. (*Do not allow "on the web page"*)
Description: Indicates that an EV (Extended Validation) SSL connection has been established, which verifies the identity of the web site.

Do not allow:

- "Tick icon (or similar) next to web site name in search results" – this only indicates site may be free of malware.
- "Uses official logos and brand names" – as phishing sites can also illegally use these.
- "Only used well-known brands" – as phishing sites often imitate these.
- Any symbols (e.g padlock) or words ("Security Verified") appearing within the actual web page content.

Award 1 mark for the method identified and 1 mark for a description of how it indicates the site is secure.

c)

Grade according to the 4 mark Explanation rubric on page 140.

Possible answers include:

- Digital signatures authenticate the organisation running the web site you are visiting.
- The organisation obtains a digital certificate from a digital certificate authority (such as VeriSign) by providing evidence of their identity.
- Upon visiting the organisation's site, your browser checks its digital certificate and indicates (e,g. in the status or address bar) the organisation is genuine.
- This reduces phishing attacks because an imitation site may use an organisation's logos and names, but it will not have access to their digital certificate.

Chapter 6
Multimedia

Chapter 6 Solutions

Exercise 6-1

(These answers are already in the text). Only the watch image is a photograph. The mountains, eggs, and car were all generated using computer graphics software.

Exercise 6-2

Grade according to the rubric on page 127.

Exercise 6-3

This is a practical exercise to familiarise students with graphics manipulation software.

Exercise 6-4

This is a practical exercise to familiarise students with graphics manipulation software.

Exercise 6-5

Possible answers include:

Scenario 1
Arguments in favour of the changes

- The subjects (presumably) do not have red-eyes naturally—making these alternations restores the image to its "correct" state
- The changes are minor—the "content" of the image is not being changed per se
- There is no attempt to mislead

Arguments against the changes

- Any change to an image alters its integrity. In certain situations this may mean the integrity of the entire image is called into account

Scenario 2
Arguments in favour of the changes

- It is better to show "some" of the reality of war than nothing at all
- The newspaper is governed by law and so cannot show the complete images

Arguments against the changes

- There are alternatives to editing the images: other images which are less graphic (but unaltered) could be used instead, or images could be cropped to discard the offensive material.
- Changes to these images could call into question the integrity of all the newspaper's images, harming its reputation.
- A false perception of the war could be created in the minds of the viewers (believing it to be less horrific than it is).

Scenario 3
Arguments in favour of the changes

- Victims often feel scared or ashamed; hiding their identity in this way can help encourage them to speak out.
- Including a picture (even if pixelated) reminds readers that there is a human victim behind the crime (which may improve response rate).

Arguments against the changes

- It may be easier to make false accusations against a person if you are anonymous.
- The victim's identity may still be at risk if the alterations are insufficient or can be undone (technology exists to "undo" certain types of images distortions like this).

Scenario 4
This is perhaps the most controversial of the scenarios.

Arguments in favour of the changes

- The models whose images are altered may have given permission for the changes.
- The problems often associated with such image manipulations have not been scientifically proven.
- The images are not necessarily intended to represent reality.

Arguments against the changes

- As many (young) people look up to these people, it may encourage them to strive for unobtainable images of themselves.
- This may lead to psychological consequences
- This may lead to unhealthy practises such as inappropriate levels of exercise or unhealthy eating practices.

This exercise should be marked according to the ITGS generic mark band for SL and HL Paper 1 Part (c). This can be found online in the ITGS Specimen Papers.

Exercise 6-6

a)

16 colour images use 4 bits per pixel

      640 × 480 = 307,200 pixels

      307,200 × 4 = 1,228,800 bits

      = 153,600 bytes

      = 153.6 kilobytes

(150 kilobytes if dividing by 1024 instead of 1000)

Award 1 mark for the correct answer and 1 mark for the correct working / calculations.

b)

256 colour images use 8 bits (1 byte) per pixel

      1024 × 768 = 786,432 pixels

      786,432 × 1 = 786,432 bytes

      =768.4 kilobytes

      (768 kilobytes if dividing by 1024 instead of 1000)

Award 1 mark for the correct answer and 1 mark for the correct working / calculations.

c)

True colour implies 24 bits (3 bytes) per pixel.

4 megapixels implies 4,000,000 pixels (image dimensions are irrelevant).

      4,000,000 × 3 = 12,000,000 bytes

      =12 megabytes

(11.44 megabytes if dividing by 1024 instead of 1000)

Award 1 mark for the correct answer and 1 mark for the correct working / calculations.

d)

Television pictures are broadcast in true colour (24 bits / 3 bytes per pixel).

      A full high definition image is 1920 × 1080 pixels:

      1920 × 1080 = 2,073,600 pixels

      2,073,600 × 3 = 6,220,800 bytes

      = 6,220 kilobytes

      (6,075 kilobytes if dividing by 1024 instead of 1000)

      = 6.07 megabytes

      (5.93 megabytes if dividing by 1024 instead of 1000)

Alternatively, if a student takes high definition to be 1280 × 720 pixels:

      1280 × 720 = 921,600 pixels

      2,073,600 × 3 = 2,764,800 bytes

      = 2,764 kilobytes

      (2,700 kilobytes if dividing by 1024 instead of 1000)

      = 2.76 megabytes

      (2.63 megabytes if dividing by 1024 instead of 1000)

Award 1 mark for the correct answer and 1 mark for the correct working / calculations.

Exercise 6-7

A single high definition frame requires 6,220,800 bytes of storage (see exercise 6-6 part d above).

1 second of film therefore requires:

      6,220,800 × 29 = 180,403,200 bytes

In a two hour film there are 60 × 60 × 2 = 7,200 seconds

Storage space required is therefore:

      180,403,200 × 7,200 = 1,298,903,040,000 bytes

      1,298,903,040 kilobytes

      1,298,903 megabytes

      1,298.9 gigabytes

      1.30 terabytes

Note: this appears incorrect (even a Blu-ray disk cannot hold this much data, for example) – but remember that this calculation deals with uncompressed data. Page 124 discusses how this problem is solved.

Award 1 mark for the correct answer and 1 mark for the correct working / calculations.

Exercise 6-8

Grade according to the 4 mark Explanation rubric on page 140.

Sample answer:

The second image (on the right) would likely achieve better compression using lossless compression. This is because the image is cartoon-style and therefore contains large areas of the same colour [*NB: do not allow "similar colour"*]. The data to represent these areas can easily be compressed. In contrast, the photograph of the dog contains many areas where adjacent pixels are similar but not identical colours. This makes lossless compression much harder because there are fewer areas of repeated data.

Exercise 6-9

a)

Commercial printing is typically done at 300 pixels per inch. Therefore:

24 inches × 300 = 7,200 pixels across
16 inches × 300 = 4,800 pixels across

7,200 × 4,800 = 34,560,000 pixels
(which is about 34.5 megapixels)

Award 1 mark for the correct answer and 1 mark for the correct working / calculations.

b)

2240 × 1680 is a common resolution for 4 megapixel cameras.

2240 / 300 = 7.46 inches
1680 / 300 = 5.6 inches

Award 1 mark for the correct answer and 1 mark for the correct working / calculations.

c)

Assuming the output is at 150 PPI:

1600 / 150 = 10.6 inches
1200 / 150 = 8 inches

Award 1 mark for the correct answer and 1 mark for the correct working / calculations.

Exercise 6-10

The bar graph produced will depend on the precise file formats the student selected (and to a certain extent on the image content too). However, as a general rule:

- Uncompressed formats such as BMP should appear with the largest file sizes.
- Lossless formats such as TIF, PNG, and GIF should appear with "medium" file sizes.
- Lossy formats such as JPEG should appear with much smaller file sizes, especially with high compression ratios.
- Proprietary formats such as Adobe Photoshop's PSD will vary according to the image complexity, but are likely to be on the larger end of the scale due to the additional data they store (for example undo lists, history, layers).

Exercise 6-11

This is a practical exercise to familiarise students with 3D graphics software. After the exercise students should come to understand that, in general:

a) Simple objects with largely "rectangular" geometry and many straight edges are relatively easy to create.
b) Recreating familiar places may be relatively easy, but difficulties such as scale and adding fine detail can arise.
c) Natural objects with many curved or uneven surfaces, or a lot of fine detail, are much more difficult to recreate realistically. This can lead to a discussion of the difficulty involved in many movie special effects where facial movements, clothing, and hair must all be created.

Exercise 6-12

This exercise is intended to help students apply the concepts they have learnt throughout the chapter (including in exercise 6-11). Students should look for examples of actors, effects, locations, and props which may have been enhanced using digital technology or may exist only as digital versions.

Exercise 6-13

1) F
2) D
3) B
4) H
5) C
6) I
7) A
8) G
9) E

Exercise 6-14

Possible answers include:

- Edited images of sports stars and models may create unrealistic expectations in young people who try to achieve similar bodies—this can lead to unhealthy lifestyles (over-exercising, poor eating habits).
- Many magazines contain heavily edited images that reach a large audience—thus potentially affecting many people.
- It is often difficult to determine whether images have been changed, making them more believable.
- Editors may be tempted to allow altered images to increase sales; legislation could make the same rules

apply to everyone.

- Warnings may be ineffective as they do not give a clear indication of the extent of the alteration (the original image is not visible).

This exercise should be marked according to the ITGS generic mark band for SL and HL Paper 1 Part (c). This can be found online in the ITGS Specimen Papers.

Exercise 6-15
Grade according to the rubric on page 128.

Exercise 6-16
Possible answers include:
Reason: The company may already have staff familiar with these types of media.
Explanation: There will be no need to search for and hire new members of staff who have the skills to work with Web 2.0 media.

Reason: Web 2.0 media may not be suitable for the task or audience.
Explanation: Word processors, desktop publishing software, and even presentations may be able to communicate more detailed information than posts on social networks or blogs.

Reason: There may be concerns about data ownership.
Explanation: Many web 2.0 tools are hosted in the cloud and companies may be unwilling to store their data remotely for fear of privacy breaches, security issues, or the vendor going bust.

Reason: The company may be worried about unauthorised / unofficial posts by employees.
Explanation: It is harder for companies to control the posts their employees make to their social media channels.

Reason: There may be a fear of negative comments.
Explanation: Unhappy customers (or rivals posing as such) could post negative comments on social networks which can harm a company's image.

Reason: It may be hard to maintain the company or brand's "look and feel" with web 2.0 tools.
Explanation: Not all web 2.0 tools can be customised by the user to match their desired layout, colours, fonts, and other characteristics which together form the company's brand image.

Award 1 mark for identifying the advantage and 1 mark for the explanation, up to 4 marks.

Exercise 6-17
Grade according to the rubric on page 129.
Presentation design assessed should include:
- Appropriate presentation length
- Using slides with appropriate, effective images
- Using a small selection of fonts
- Using a small selection of slide transitions
- A consistent approach to design (colour, transitions, fonts, and other elements)
- Appropriate amounts of text on slides
- Appropriate use of colours / clearly visible text
- No errors in spelling or grammar

Presenters' skills assessed should include:
- Speaking clearly and with confidence
- Limited use of notes for prompting (not reading)
- Facing the audience
- Not reading slides to the audience
- Non-speaking group members are not a distraction
- Good coordinated team work

Exercise 6-18
a)
i)
Possible answers include:
- 3GP
- AVI
- FLV (Flash Video)
- MPEG / MPG
- MPEG4 / MP4
- MOV (Apple QuickTime)
- WMV (Windows Media Video)

ii)
Possible answers include:
- Image resolution—higher resolutions allow more detail to be visible in the image
- Compression—higher levels of (lossy) compression discard minor details in return for smaller file sizes.
- Colour depth—higher colour depths allow more colours, allowing it to more closely resemble real life.

Award 1 mark for identifying the factor and 1 mark for the description, up to 4 marks.

Do not allow 'file format' without a discussion of compression.

b)

- The user selects a compression level, which is a trade off between detail and file size
- The compression algorithm discards certain data (for example, subtle colour changes) according to the compression level chosen by the user
- The compression algorithm looks for patterns of continuous (repeated) data in the image
- These areas are then saved to disk in a compressed form

Award 1 mark for each step, up to 4 marks.

c)

Possible answers include:

Advantages:

- Virtual actors do not get sick or need time off work
- Virtual actors do not get tired, threaten to strike, or have personality conflicts with other actors or crew members.
- Digital technology allows the creation of effects that would otherwise be very hard or impossible to create—for example, characters morphing into others, monsters, and alien creatures.
- Virtual actors cannot get injured—making them ideal "stunt doubles".
- Virtual actors can film as many takes as required without complaint.
- Virtual acts can be reused—for example, in publicity events, sequels, and other material without the financial or time constraints of human actors.

Disadvantages:

- Even with modern technology it can be difficult to create certain items digitally—for example, hair and facial expressions.
- Virtual actors have no intelligence—every move must be programmed, which takes great skill.
- Human actors may lose their jobs.
- Legal issues can arise if virtual actors are clones of human actors—copyright and intellectual property rights may be unclear.

This exercise should be marked according to the ITGS generic mark band for SL and HL Paper 1 Part (c). This can be found online in the ITGS Specimen Papers.

Exercise 6-19

a)

i)

Possible answers include:

- DOC / DOCX (Microsoft Word)
- ODF (Open Document Format)
- PDF (Portable Document Format)
- RTF (Rich Text Format)
- TXT (Plain text)

ii)

Possible answers include:

- Word processing software is line-oriented whereas desktop publishing software is page oriented, giving greater control over page layout.
- Desktop publishing software has features to prepare documents for commercial / professional printing—word processing software typically does not.
- Desktop publishing software offers more advanced text control than word processing software—such as leading, kerning, and spacing.

Award 1 mark for identifying the difference and 1 mark for the expansion, up to 4 marks.

b)

Possible answers include:

- Documents are typically non-editable.
- Documents look exactly the same on screen as in print, even if specialist or unusual fonts are used.
- PDF is a common file format and PDF viewing software is free to download.
- Documents can be protected using Digital Rights Management (DRM) - for example, to prevent printing.
- Documents are compressed to achieve relatively small file sizes.
- Documents can be digitally signed to verify their authenticity.
- PDF documents allow interactive fields so only specific areas of the document can be edited.

Grade according to the 6 mark Explanation rubric on page 141.

c)

Possible answers include:

In favour of paper leaflets

- The business may already have the skills to create paper promotional materials—but not those for web based material.
- The cost of photocopying leaflets may be less than the cost of web site setup, development, and hosting.

- The service (dry cleaning) may be one that people do not typically look online for, but rely on word of mouth.

In favour of a web site:
- A wider audience can be reached since web sites are global.
- Advertising can be targeted to specific groups of people.
- It is easier to assess the effectiveness of campaigns—for example, measuring customer conversion rate.
- Social features could be harnessed to enable users to recommend the business to potential new customers.
- Can open a communication channel with customers to answer their questions and listen to their requests.

This exercise should be marked according to the ITGS generic mark band for SL and HL Paper 1 Part (c). This can be found online in the ITGS Specimen Papers.

Exercise 6-20

a)

i)

DPI (Dots Per Inch) refers to the number of dots an output device such as a printer produces in one physical inch *[1 mark]* which has a direct effect on the quality of the output. *[1 mark]*

ii)

Possible answers include:
- File upload—the agency could provide a web page which allows the user to select a file and upload it directly to the agency.
- Email attachment—the agency may have an email address dedicated to accepting images by email attachment.
- Social network site—the user could upload the image onto a social network and grant the agency access by 'tagging' them or some similar mechanism.
- FTP (File Transfer Protocol) - the agency could set up an FTP server that allows submissions to be uploaded into a particular directory.

Award 1 mark for the method identified and 1 mark for a description, up to 4 marks.

b)

Possible answers include:
- Readers may be the only source of content for certain events (such as photographs of the Hudson river plane crash).
- Readers may provide a unique personal insight into events.
- The cost of such images may be lower than those from traditional photo agencies.
- It creates audience engagement which can increase the number of readers.

Grade according to the 6 mark Explanation rubric on page 141.

c)

Possible answers include:
- Intellectual property and copyright issues—ensuring that the person submitting the work is the copyright holder.
- Liability issues—ensuring that the news agency is not liable if the content is deemed to be offensive, inappropriate, or illegal.
- Quality issues—ensuring that submitted material is of a sufficiently high quality to be published.
- Authenticity issues—for example, ensuring that user generated photographs are genuine and have not been manipulated.
- Issues related to appropriate behaviour—for example, rules in user forums or comments sections to govern abuse, swearing, or other inappropriate behaviour.

This exercise should be marked according to the ITGS generic mark band for SL and HL Paper 1 Part (c). This can be found online in the ITGS Specimen Papers.

Chapter 7
Databases

Chapter 7 Solutions

Exercise 7-1

a) Student identification number

Do not allow: Student name, telephone number, tutor group, date of birth or similar non-unique fields.

b) Bar code number / production identification number

Do not allow: product name, price or similar non-unique fields.

c) Employee number

Do not allow: name, telephone number, address, or similar non-unique fields.

d) Bank account number

Do not allow: Name of account holder (since one holder can have multiple accounts) or similar non-unique fields.

Exercise 7-2

This is a practical exercise to familiarise students with database software. Ideal data types for fields are given below (names may vary slightly depending upon the database software used):

- Book title - *Text*
- Author first name - *Text*
- Author second name - *Text*
- Publisher - *Text*
- Publisher country - *Text*
- Pages - *Number*
- Date of birth -*Date*
- Date of birth - *Date*
- Nationality - *Text*
- Book language - *Text*
- Original language - *Text*
- Year - *Date*
- Genre - *Text*
- Paperback – *Boolean (Yes/No)*
- Topic - *Text*

Exercise 7-3

Possible answers include:

Advantages:

- Large amounts of data can be stored in a small physical space.

- Data can easily be copied – for example, for backup purposes.
- Multiple users can access the data simultaneously.
- The data can easily be accessed from separate geographical locations without having to physically retrieve the data.
- Access levels can be implemented to allow some users to see some parts of the data but not others.
- Records can easily be transmitted to third parties – for example, if a student moves school their records can be sent with them.
- Automatic reports and alerts can be configured – for example, to automatically alert staff to students who have missed a certain number of days, or students who were recorded present but have not attended class.

Disadvantages:

- Security concerns may exist – for example if theft occurs, extremely large amounts of data can be lost at once (much more than is possible with paper records).
- Privacy concerns may exist if large amounts of data are collected and held for a long time – especially if this is done without the data subject's knowledge.
- Privacy concerns may exist if computerised techniques such as data mining are used.

This exercise should be marked according to the ITGS generic mark band for SL and HL Paper 1 Part (c). This can be found online in the ITGS Specimen Papers.

Exercise 7-4

This is a practical exercise to familiarise students with database software. The normalised database should look like that in figure 7-7 on page 149 of the textbook.

Exercise 7-5

a)

Fields that contain needlessly repeated data (redundant data):

- Head of Year (determined by the grade field)
- Registration tutor (determined by the grade field)
- Registration room (determined by the grade field)

Fields that contain data repeated with reason:

- Grade
- Prefect

- First name (contains no repeated data in this example – but could do so).
- Second name (contains no repeated data in this example – but could do so).

b)
The data should be normalised into two separate tables. There is nothing to gain from separating the Head of Year field into its own table unless additional fields dependent on it are added (for example, the head of year's telephone number). PK indicates Primary Key and FK indicates Foreign Key.

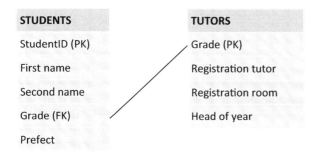

STUDENTS	TUTORS
StudentID (PK)	Grade (PK)
First name	Registration tutor
Second name	Registration room
Grade (FK)	Head of year
Prefect	

Exercise 7-6

Students should take the basic database structure from exercise 7-4 (figure 7-7) and add two additional tables for 'Orders' and 'Customers'. The resultant database should look like figure 7-1 below.

Exercise 7-7

The queries' precise output will depend on the sample records used by the students. The required criteria are:

a)
- Books.Title—Show
- Books.Genre—Show
- Authors.Second Name = "Ed Viesturs"

b)
- Books.Original language = "English"
- Books.Book language = Not null

c)
- Books.Year = 1998

d)
- Books.Pages >250

e)
- Books.Publisher country = "UK"

f)
- Books.Title—Show
- Authors.Nationality = "Canada"

g)
- Books.Topic = "Mountaineering" OR "Hiking" OR "camping"

Figure 7-1 Normalised database solution for exercise 7-6

AUTHORS	BOOKS		ORDERS	CUSTOMERS
*AuthorID	*BookID		*Order Number	*CustomerID
First Name	AuthorID		Order Date	First name
Second Name	Publisher		CustomerID	Second name
Date of Birth	Title		BookID	Address
Date of Death	Pages	PUBLISHER	Price	Telephone
Nationality	Book language	*Publisher	Shipped Date	
	Original language	Publisher Country		
	Year			
	Genre			
	Paperback			

Exercise 7-8

The queries' output will depend on the sample records used by the students and the parameters they input. The required criteria are:

a) Books.Publisher = ["Enter the publisher name"]
b) Books.Topic = ["Enter the topic"]
c) Books.Author second name = ["Enter name"]

Exercise 7-9

The queries' output will depend on the sample records used by the students. The required criteria are:

a)
- Books.Title—Show
- Orders.Order date—Show
- Customers.Customer second name = ["Enter name"]

b)
- Books.Title—Show
- Orders.Order date > CurDate() - 7

c)
- Orders.Order date < CurDate() - 30
- Orders.Shipped date = Null

Exercise 7-10

Grade according to the rubric on page 130.

Exercise 7-11

See figure 7-2 below for solution.

Note:

Character checks are implicitly performed by certain data types—for example, a numeric field forbids letters and symbols.

Presence checks have only been indicated for fields deemed 'required' - i.e. those that should not be left blank.

Exercise 7-12

a)

Possible answers include:

- Users agree to this data collection when they sign up for the site (it is listed in the terms and conditions / the privacy policy).
- The collection of such data is the price users pay for using the system without charge.
- Targeted advertisements may be less annoying than generalised advertisements.
- Users can opt-out by deleting their account.
- Not all social networks delete account data when a count is removed.
- Users may not be aware of the precise data being collected about them (privacy policies are often not explicit).
- Users may not be aware of the length of time data about them is held (privacy policies are often quite vague).

Figure 7-2 Completed table for exercise 7-11

Field	Example	Range Check	Length Check	Character check	Presence check	Consistency check	Check digit
Title	If This is a Man		Y	Y	Y		
Author	Primo Levi		Y	Y	Y		
Publication date	1958	Y		Y	Y		
ISBN	0349100136		Y	Y	Y		Y
Normal Price	$14.99	Y		Y	Y	Y	
Sale Price	$10.99	Y		Y		Y	
Publisher	Abacus		Y				
Number of pages	129	Y		Y			
Web site	www.itgsnews.com			Y			

- Data is likely to be passed to third-parties (the advertisers) and linked with other data (data matching).
- Judgements may be made about the user without their knowledge / users may not be able to see what decisions are made about them.

b)
Possible answers include:
- Medical / prescription data is regarded as highly sensitive.
- Patients' names and contact details are removed from the data before it is shared.
- Even 'anonymous' data can sometimes reveal a large amount of information about the data subject (if it did not, why would advertisers want it?).
- Prescription data can easily be linked to other data bases (data matching) to reveal further trends.
- Drug manufacturers use this information to market drugs to specific doctors—potentially breaching the patient-doctor relationship and increasing drug costs.

c)
Possible answers include:
- The use of this data has the potential to benefit everyone; reduced fraud means lower costs and potential lower taxes.
- The data being examined is inherently personally identifiable data.
- Data mining must be used on everybody's data in order to identify just a very small number of fraudsters.
- The ratio of fraudsters identified compared to the number of innocent people's data that is checked may be very low.
- Data mining has the potential to throw up false positives if the data sets are not adequately prepared.
- The data being used may not have been originally collected for that purpose; the data subjects may not have agreed to its use.
- The sharing of data with other government departments increases the risk of security and privacy beaches.
- There may be concerns that government will use this data for other purposes.

d)
Possible answers include:
- If insurance companies can reduce their costs they can improve cover / reduce costs for their customers.
- Results from data mining may not be 100% accurate.
- Health data is regarded as highly sensitive.
- If they need health insurance, customers may feel forced into allowing access to their sensitive data.
- Insurance companies may pass this data on to other companies (for example, advertising and marketing companies).

This exercise should be marked according to the generic ITGS extended response rubric for SL and HL Paper 1. This can be found in the ITGS Specimen Papers.

Exercise 7-13
1) D
2) A
3) F
4) B
5) C
6) E

A common mistake here is to mix up Foreign Key (1) and Secondary Key (3).

Exercise 7-14
Possible answers include:
Characteristic: Computer data can be invisibly copied
Explanation: the original copy is left intact, meaning the theft is less likely to be noticed than if paper records were taken.

Characteristic: Data consumes little physical space
Explanation: A thief can steal thousands or millions of records and easily transport them (for example, on a flash drive).

Characteristic: Computer database are often accessed remotely
Explanation: This makes the detection of intruders harder and there may be no physical signs of their presence.

Award 1 mark for the characteristic and 1 mark for the explanation, up to 4 marks.

Exercise 7-15

Grade according to the rubric and sample diagram on page 131.

Exercise 7-16

a) SELECT product_name FROM products WHERE manufacturer = "ABC Electronics"

b) SELECT review_text FROM reviews WHERE product_code = "E9483"

c) SELECT product_name FROM products WHERE release_date > Now() - 7

d) SELECT product_name FROM orders WHERE orders.customer_id = (SELECT orders.customer_id FROM orders WHERE orders.product_id = 1)

e) UPDATE products SET price="9.95" WHERE name = "Jeans" AND colour="Blue" AND size = "small"

f) DELETE FROM transactions WHERE date < CURDATE() - 1825

Note: Part (d) assumes that the current product being viewed has a product_id of 1.

Exercise 7-17

a)

i)

Data matching is the combination of database records from several separate databases [1 mark] in order to create a larger body of information on a person or group of people. [1 mark]

ii)

Possible answers include:

- Full name (text) - name of passenger, used to check no-fly lists.
- Address (text) - full address of passenger, used to determine identity.
- Nationality (text) - contains the traveller's nationality, used to determine identity and assign 'risk score'.
- Passport number (text) - contains the passport number of the passenger, used to determine identity.
- Date of birth (date / time) - the passenger's date of birth, used to determine identity.
- Place of birth (text) - used to determine identity and assign 'risk score'.
- Gender (Boolean) - used to determine identity and assign 'risk score'.
-

Award 1 mark for the field name and 1 mark for the data type, up to 4 marks.

b)

Possible answers include:

- Travel history could be examined—this might reveal 'suspicious' travel in the past.
- Credit rating information —could help establish a passengers history and verify their identity.
- Purchase history—could be used to establish a passenger's "roots in the community".
- Library records—could be used to establish if a passenger has "subversive" interests.

Grade according to the 6 mark Explanation rubric on page 141.

c)

Possible answers include:

Arguments in favour

- The system is automated—it can process many more passengers than human based systems.
- The system can detect 'hidden' threats that may be missed by a human security screener.
- The mere presence of the system may deter would-be attackers.

Arguments against

- Data matching and data mining techniques may be considered a breach of privacy.
- It is not clear what data is collected or how it is used—a clear privacy issue.
- Integrity—the number of false positives is relatively high—these cause serious inconvenience.
- Details of the system are secret—its accuracy, effectiveness, and fairness are not open to public scrutiny.
- Predicting "likely" terrorists is very hard or impossible—the task may simply be a waste of time and money.

This exercise should be marked according to the generic ITGS extended response rubric for SL and HL Paper 1. This can be found in the ITGS Specimen Papers.

Exercise 7-18

a)

i)

A primary key is a field in a database table [1 mark] which is unique for every record in that table. [1 mark]

ii)

A query should be created with the following criteria:

- City = "Washington D.C"
- Conviction = "Assault"

Award 1 for identifying the field and 1 mark for the correct criteria, up to 4 marks.

b)

Possible answers include:

- During data entry, the data could be entered twice—this would reduce human transcription errors.
- The database contents could be cross-checked with paper documents such as passports and police reports—this would reduce the likelihood of transcription errors.
- The data subject could be interviewed and asked to verify the data's accuracy—this could help ensure the data is up to date.

Grade according to the 6 mark Explanation rubric on page 141.

c)

Possible answers include:

Arguments in favour:

- This information is often publicly available already—releasing it online simply makes it more accessible.
- People might believe they have a right to know if they are living near people convicted of serious crimes.
- This information could lead to increased vigilance, improving neighbourhood safety.
- The information could lead to improved relationships with the police (increased openness and transparency).

Arguments against:

- Releasing personal details online may breach the data subject's rights to privacy.
- The offender's ability to rehabilitate himself may be harmed if his history is widely known.
- The data may encourage vigilante attacks against offenders.
- The data may provide a false sense of security—a belief that those in the database are the *only* threats in the neighbourhood.

This exercise should be marked according to the generic ITGS extended response rubric for SL and HL Paper 1. This can be found in the ITGS Specimen Papers.

Exercise 7-19

a)

i)

Possible answers include:

- Bicycle ID—Autonumber
- Bicycle make—Text
- Bicycle last location—text
- UserID—Autonumber
- User name—Text
- User account balance—currency
- Bike hire date—Date / Time
- Bike return date—Date / Time

Award 1 mark for the field and 1 mark for the correct data type, up to 4 marks.

ii)

A foreign key is a field in a database table [1 mark] that exists solely to form part of a relationship with another table [1 mark].

b)

Possible answers include:

- The database is split into multiple tables
- Each table represents a single type of entity
- Tables are related
- The database is normalised (redundant data / unnecessarily duplicated data is removed)
- Only one copy of data is stored / updated: no chance of multiple inconsistent copies of the data being stored

Grade according to the 6 mark Explanation rubric on page 141.

c)

Possible answers include:

- Security —sensitive data such as credit card numbers may be stored in the system. Access to this by unauthorised users could result in fraud being committed.
- Security—if inadequate authentication is in place or the authentication card is lost, an unauthorised user may be able to access the system and steal bicycles in the user's name.

- Privacy—personal data may be stored (such as name, address, date of birth), which needs to be adequately protected or there is a risk of identity theft.

- Privacy—additional data may be collected about the user without their knowledge—for example, a profile of their journeys could be created with data such as times and locations.

- Privacy—the cyclist's data may be transmitted or sold to third parties who may use it for other purposes (such as sending advertisements).

This exercise should be marked according to the generic ITGS extended response rubric for SL and HL Paper 1. This can be found in the ITGS Specimen Papers.

Chapter 8
Models &
Simulations

Chapter 8 Solutions

Exercise 8-1

This is a practical exercise to familiarise students with computer models.

Exercise 8-2

a) Car crash models

Possible answers include:

Processes:

- A model of human physiology (for example, skeletal structure, internal organs)
- A model of collision physics (for example, Newton's laws)
- A model of the car structure (Rigid body physics)

Do not allow "weather conditions", since these can influence whether a crash will occur, but not the result of a crash. In a car crash model a crash is assumed to occur.

Variables:

- The safety features the car has (for example, seat belts, air bags)
- The age, weight, and height of the vehicle occupants
- The speed of the vehicle(s) involved in the collision
- The type of collisions (car versus car, car versus pedestrian, side impact, head-on impact)
- The car's material and strength

Predictions:

- How will the car deform in a variety of impacts?
- What injuries will passengers suffer?
- How do safety features affect these two factors?

Decisions:

- Car manufacturers can decide the best combination of safety features for their vehicles.
- Governments can base traffic policies and laws on the results (for example, deciding to reduce speed limits to a speed shown to have a significant reduction in injuries).

b) Climate models

Possible answers include:

Processes:

- Solar energy and solar cycles
- Water evaporation
- Land carbon cycle
- Ocean carbon cycle
- Atmospheric chemistry ("Greenhouse effect")
- Natural carbon emissions
- Human carbon emissions

Variables:

- Amount of carbon dioxide released naturally
- Amount of carbon dioxide released by humans (industrial pollution, transportation).
- Natural changes in solar energy from sun

Predictions:

- Future global temperatures
- Future sea level changes
- Future changes to land (for example, desertification)
- Future weather patterns

Decisions:

- Governments can base environmental policies and laws on the results (for example, carbon dioxide emission requirements).
- Governments can prepare for possible climate change (for example, constructing sea defences in areas predicted to be at risk).

c) Earthquake models

Possible answers include:

Processes:

- Model of the physics associated with ground movement, swaying, loads, and building collapse .

Do not allow: plate tectonics, since this does not predict the effect on buildings

Variables:

- Location of fault / earthquake epicentre relative to buildings (distance and depth).
- Strength of the earthquake
- Types of building materials
- Earthquake resistant measures used in buildings
- Size, shape, and height of buildings

Predictions:

- How well buildings will survive various strengths of earthquake.
- How effective different strategies (building reinforcement, alternative construction materials, base isolation) are in preventing building damage.
- The number of possible building collapses and injuries given a specific magnitude earthquake in a specific area.
- The risk of associated effects (for example tsunamis).

Do not allow: when an earthquake will occur

Decisions:
- Governments can enact building codes that require particular earthquake-resistant features.
- Governments can locate buildings most likely to be damaged and take appropriate action.
- Governments can locate emergency rescue and medical facilities in areas where most damage is likely to occur.

d) Search and rescue models
Possible answers include:
Processes:
- Model of tides (in sea rescue models)
- Model of wind
- Model of weather (for example rain) and temperature.
- Model of human behaviour when lost (for example, staying still or continuing to move).

Variables:
- Age and fitness of the lost person
- Starting location
- Wind speed and direction
- Rescue equipment the lost person possesses
- Presence of predators in the area
- Type of terrain (forest, desert, flat, steep)

Predictions:
- Where a person may be (for example having walked, being taken by the tide, blown by the wind).
- How likely it is that an individual may have survived.

Decisions:
- Rescuers can determine the best locations to start a search.
- Rescuers can determine how long a search should continue before hope is lost.

e) Disease spread models
Possible answers include:
Processes:
- Infection processes (airborne, water-borne, STD)
- Human movement "mixing" – which determines the number of candidates for infection.

Variables:
- How infectious a disease is
- How deadly a disease is
- How frequently preventative measures are used (for example, condoms in the case of HIV).
- How many people are vaccinated against a disease

Predictions:
- How many people are likely to be infected by a disease.
- How many infected people are likely to die from a disease.
- How quickly a disease is likely to spread.

Decisions:
- Governments can decide whether or not to vaccinate people against certain diseases.
- Governments can decide what type of education / advice would be most effective in preventing disease spread.
- Governments can determine the type and quantity of medical supplies they are likely to need for a given outbreak.
- Governments can decide how best to deploy medical personnel and facilities.

f) Eco-system models
Possible answers include:
Processes:
- The food chain (which animal eats which)
- Characteristics of animals (for example, how much they eat and how frequently)
- Breeding cycle of animals (frequency and litter size)

Variables:
- Initial number of each animal / plant
- The size of the available land / sea area

Predictions:
- The numbers of each species and food source after a given time

Decisions:
- Authorities (governments, park rangers) can determine the possible impacts of introducing new species to an ecosystem
- Authorities (governments, park rangers) can determine which animals may need protection
- Authorities (governments, park rangers) can determine which animals may need controlling (for example, culling or moving to other areas)

Exercise 8-3
a)
Possible answers include:
Missing variable: Carbon dioxide absorption by nature
Possible data source: The rates of absorption by various species of plant are available in scientific literature.

Missing variable: Plant cover
Possible data source: Value could be based on past surveys of plant cover (which may be estimates).

Missing variable: Rate of forestation / deforestation
Possible data source: Value could be based on past surveys of plant cover (which may be estimates).

Missing variable: Ocean levels
Possible data source: Value could be based on historical data / research.

b)
Variables based on scientific understanding (for example rate of carbon dioxide absorption by plants) are easier to incorporate.

Possible answers include:
- Rates which change over time are difficult to implement accurately. For example the current rate of deforestation, or the current rate of carbon dioxide production can be used, but these can increase or decrease. This is particularly true if the model makes predictions about the distant future (for example 20 or 30 years ahead).
- Modelling human behaviour is difficult - it is difficult to know how people will react to various influences. For example, deforestation may continue unhindered for many years, or may decrease suddenly as humans decide it must stop.
- In other models (such as the search and rescue model) it is difficult to know how the lost person will behave – will they continue walking or stop and stay in place?

Grade according to the 4 mark Explanation rubric on page 140.

Exercise 8-4
a)
Possible answers include:
- Air resistance is not modelled (the model represents a vacuum).
- Varying air density (at different altitudes or temperatures) is not modelled.
- Cross winds are not modelled.
- The shape of the projectile is not modelled (which affects its air resistance).
- Thrust is not modelled—the projectile is simply launched.
- Varying gravity is not modelled (it changes slightly at different altitudes and at different latitudes).

b)
Possible answers include:
- Errors could occur in the construction of the model (for example, mistakes when entering the formulae).
- Errors could be made when entering data (especially constant values such as that for gravity).
- Errors could occur because our scientific understanding of processes is incomplete—for example, we do not know the role of certain gases in climate change.

Award 1 mark for the method identified and 1 mark for a description, up to 6 marks.

c)
Possible answers include:
- To solve issues of incorrect formulae, tests can be run with past data to check the model's results against known results.
- Errors in data entry could also be verified by using test data with known results (e.g. past data).
- Some errors cannot be resolved, but by being aware of the lack of understanding the model's a margin of error / confidence interval can be determined.

Grade according to the 6 mark Explanation rubric on page 141.

d)
Grade according to the 4 mark Explanation rubric on page 140.

Sample answer:
The t_step variable helps determine the accuracy of the 'impact time' result. For example, if t_step were 10 seconds, we might know the missile impacted sometime between 20 seconds and 30 seconds after launch, but we could be no more accurate. If t_step were 5 seconds, we could determine the impact time to that accuracy (e.g. between 25 seconds and 30 seconds). The higher the value for t_step, the higher the margin of error.

e)
Possible answers include:
- The model's output can be compared to the expected range of outputs—if the answers are far outside the expected range, an error is likely to have occurred.
- The models can be tested on input data for which the actual results are already known (for example, historical weather data). The real results and the model's results can then be compared to determine if there are any significant differences.
- An expert in the model's domain (such as a climate prediction expert) could assess the model's results.

Grade according to the 4 mark Explanation rubric on page 140.

Exercise 8-5
Possible answers include:
Advantages:
- Models allow scenarios to be tested that would be too expensive to try in real life.
- Models allow scenarios to be tested that would be too dangerous to try in real life.
- Models allow time to be slowed down to investigate very quick phenomenon (e.g. nuclear reactions).
- Models allow time to be speeded up to investigate and make predictions about the future.
- The variables in a model can be changed to allow "what if" scenarios to be tested.
- Some tests (for example drug or genetic research) may be unethical to person on humans or animals, so models can be used instead.

Disadvantages:
- By their very nature, models can only model concepts and phenomenon that we understand sufficiently to codify in a computer program.
- Inaccurate results from models may lead to false directions of investigation or misunderstanding.
- Certain types of phenomenon (such as human behaviour) are very hard to model mathematically, limiting the usefulness of models.

This exercise should be marked according to the generic ITGS extended response rubric for SL and HL Paper 1. This can be found in the ITGS Specimen Papers.

Exercise 8-6
a)
i) A computer model is a computer program [1 mark] that uses a mathematical representation of a real world idea, concept, or phenomenon. [1 mark]

ii)
Possible answers include:
- Incoming energy—The amount of the sun's energy that reaches the atmosphere.
- Earth's albedo—the reflectivity of the Earth's surface.
- Cloud albedo—the reflectivity of the clouds.
- Terrain type (ocean or land, and type of land) which affects carbon dioxide uptake and solar energy absorption.
- Greenhouse gas levels—the levels of carbon dioxide and similar gasses in the atmosphere.

Award 1 mark for the variable and 1 mark for the description, up to 4 marks.

b)
Possible answers include:
- Patterns may be easier to spot graphically than in a table of numbers – for example, a series of repeating numbers is harder to spot than a series of repeating colours. This can help users spot phenomenon that might otherwise be missed.
- Anomalies may be easier to spot – for example, in a table of figures a few extreme values can be hard to see, but in graphical output they may be represented in a different colour. This can help users spot phenomenon that might otherwise be missed.
- Very large amounts of data can be represented in a smaller amount of space: for example, hundreds of rows of data representing multiple weeks could be represented using an animated diagram.
- Graphical output may be more suitable to the audience – for example, the audience may be non-technical and require only an overview of the data rather than the precise figures. Graphical output can make it easier for them to understand.

Grade according to the 6 mark Explanation rubric on page 141.

c)
Possible answers include:
Advantages:
- Models allow "what-if" scenarios to be tested. These may be too expensive, time consuming, or impractical to try in real life.
- Model 'time' can be speeded up to predict the effects far into the future.
- Multiple hypotheses can be tested to determine the one with the best possible results.
- There is no risk to the environment or people if poor policies are tested.

Disadvantages:
- Models are never 100% accurate—variables and processes may be missing as a result of our lack of scientific understanding.
- Inaccurate results could lead to the implementation of poor policies.
- The model might not consider certain events that can affect the climate (such as volcanic eruptions).
- Certain behaviours are hard to model but may affect the actual output (for example, if the level of human-produced carbon dioxide changes in the future).

This exercise should be marked according to the generic ITGS extended response rubric for SL and HL Paper 1. This can be found in the ITGS Specimen Papers.

Exercise 8-7

a)

i)

Parallel processing is the idea of using multiple processors [1 mark] to perform several calculations simultaneously, improving overall computing speed. [1 mark]

ii)

Possible answers include:

- Projector or screen –used to display images of the race track and surrounding environment.
- Force feedback (for example in the steering wheel) – used to provide a more realistic feel to the steering by adding resistance to the user's input.
- Speakers – used to produce the sounds of the engine, tyres, etc.
- Full motion platform – used to roll, lift, and raise move the entire simulator unit (including the user) to reproduce the forces on the driver associated with driving a car.

Award 1 mark for the device and 1 mark for the description, up to 4 marks.

b)

Possible answers include:

- They can practise on any circuit at any time – even if the circuit is closed or in use for other purposes, the team can still practise driving around a virtual version of it.
- Any weather conditions can be simulated – this allows the team to practise (for example in wet conditions) without having to wait for the weather to change.
- Running costs can be reduced – the team does not need to transport vehicles, equipment, and personnel to the circuit, pay for staff's accommodation and food, spend money on fuel for the racing cars, or pay to hire a real circuit.
- No chance of crashes or accidents – this saves money because there will be no damaged cars to repair, and improves safety because there is no chance of the driver being hurt.

Grade according to the 6 mark Explanation rubric on page 141.

c)

Possible answers include:

- A variety of conditions can be tested (for example wet weather or different car setups) reducing the need to practise those situations in real life.
- The simulator uses real-life input and output hard-ware to make it as realistic as possible, giving a more immersive experience.
- Any track that has been programmed into the simulator can be practised, without the need to travel.
- The underlying mathematical models will never be 100% accurate, meaning the model still differs from reality.
- A simulator never gives a fully accurate experience of a real life experience (for example, the physical forces will not be acting on the driver as the car accelerates and corners.
- The stress of dangerous situations is absent, reducing the realism.
- Circuits can only be practised if their data has been programmed into the simulator—this can be a time consuming and expensive process.

This exercise should be marked according to the generic ITGS extended response rubric for SL and HL Paper 1. This can be found in the ITGS Specimen Papers.

Exercise 8-8

a)

i)

Possible answers include:

- ABS
- AVERAGE
- COS
- COUNT
- DATE
- IF
- MAX
- MIN
- SIN
- SUM
- TAN

ii)

Relative cell referencing is a cell reference that changes when the formula using it is copied or moved to another cell. [1 mark] For example, =A1+B1 becomes =A2+B2 when moved one row down. [1 mark]

Absolute cell referencing is a cell reference that does not change, [1 mark] even when the formula using it is copied or moved to another cell, and is denoted using the dollar sign ($). [1 mark]

b)

Possible answers include:

- Number of assembly lines—the number of assembly lines manufacturing items during the shift.
- Component made by each assembly line—the type of component each assembly line creates this shift.
- Assembly line speed / rate of production—the number of components each assembly line can produce each shift.
- Required number of each component—the number of each component that is required by the manager.
- Time taken to manufacture each part—each part may take a different amount of time to complete.
- Quantity of each part required for a given toy—so the factory knows how many of each to produce.

Award 1 mark for the variable and 1 mark for the description, up to 6 marks.

c)

Possible answers include:

- The model allows the manager to quickly test various scenarios and combinations of parts to manufacture, without having to commit resources.
- The model could provide production targets which the manager could use to assess the efficiency of the operation.
- The software model may contain errors (bugs) which prevent it from producing accurate results.
- The model cannot account for unpredictable phenomenon—such assembly line breakages which may delay production.
- The model may make certain assumptions—such as the speed of a worker—but these can vary greatly depending on the day and are difficult to predict.
- The model may fail to take into account some variables—such as the time taken to setup the assembly lines to manufacture different parts.

This exercise should be marked according to the generic ITGS extended response rubric for SL and HL Paper 1. This can be found in the ITGS Specimen Papers.

Exercise 8-9

This is a practical exercise to familiarise students with using spreadsheet software to create computer models.

Chapter 9
Business

Chapter 9 Solutions

Exercise 9-1
Grade according to the rubric on page 132.

Note that students should cover how monitoring technology will be used by the employers; not how employees are allowed to use technology such as the Internet at work.

Exercise 9-2
a)
Possible answers include:
- Occupations where employees deal with sensitive data and employers wish to ensure company procedures for handling it are being followed.
- Occupations that involve a lot of telephone or email interaction with customers—data from these interactions can be used to improve company performance.
- Situations where new employees are being trained and employers wish to monitor their performance.
- Occupations where worker safety may be at immediate risk—monitoring can help spot potential hazards.

Award 1 mark for the description and 1 mark for a suitable example, up to 4 marks.

b)
Possible answers include:
- Monitoring employees (without their knowledge) can give employees a clearer idea of reality than if employees are aware of monitoring and therefore acting differently.
- Monitoring without knowledge may be considered a serious breach of the employees' privacy.
- Monitoring employees (with their knowledge) can reduce staff morale—employers may prefer secret monitoring.
- Legally requiring notification of monitoring would ensure employees are aware that data is being collected about them—this may give them a chance to leave if they feel it is a violation of privacy.
- In some countries (for example the US) rights to privacy do not extend to the workplace.

Grade according to the 6 mark Discuss rubric on page 142.

c)
Possible answers include:
- The equipment being used belongs to the employer, suggesting they have a right to monitor its use.

- Employees may unwittingly introduce security risks into the system (for example, via infected attachments in personal email)—the employer needs to prevent this.
- Employees may deliberately or accidentally leak sensitive company or customer data via personal email—the employer needs to protect this data.
- Employees do have some rights to privacy in the workplace and may, for example, be on an official break while using their personal email.

Grade according to the 6 mark Explanation rubric on page 142.

d)
Possible answers include:
- Monitoring can make employees stressed, which can reduce the quality of their work.
- Monitoring (if employees are aware of it) can reduce time wasted due to distraction.
- Monitoring data can be used to find inefficient business practises and optimise them.
- Monitoring data can be used in employee performance reports.

This exercise should be marked according to the generic ITGS extended response rubric for SL and HL Paper 1. This can be found in the ITGS Specimen Papers.

e)
Possible answers include:
- Telephone conversation monitoring is often useful for assessing customer satisfaction and looking for ways to improve the business.
- Telephone conversation monitoring may be legally required in some sectors, or may be used to ensure employees follow the law and company policies.
- Keystroke loggers can record essential information—such as passwords that may be needed if staff leave suddenly—but will also capture any private information typed on the computer.
- Monitoring of files copied and opened may be essential to ensure the privacy and security of the company's data is not violated.
- Monitoring of printing can be useful to avoid company waste.
- Monitoring of open applications or window titles may reveal employees who are wasting large amounts of time.
- Monitoring of software installations may be essential to ensure malware or unlicensed software are not installed on the company's computers.

This exercise should be marked according to the generic ITGS extended response rubric for SL and HL Paper 1. This can be found in the ITGS Specimen Papers.

Exercise 9-3
Possible answers include:
Disadvantages for employers
- There is an increased risk of data security and privacy breaches through lost or stolen laptops.
- Additional expenses may be required to purchase mobile computing devices.
- They have less control over how their employees utilise their time—there is a potential for the employee's efficiency to drop.

Benefits for employers
- Employees can be hired from a wide geographical region—this enables them to find the people with the most suitable skills.
- Employees can remain employed even if they have commitments such as children or relatives for whom they must care.
- Employees can work even in the event of disruptions such as natural disasters or transport strikes.
- There will be reduced overheads—expenditure on rent, power, and other consumables will be reduced.
- Employee's flexible working hours may mean more work is performed.

Benefits for employees
- Flexible working hours allow employees to fit work around any other commitments they may have.
- Time and money is saved if commuting is avoided.

This exercise should be marked according to the generic ITGS extended response rubric for SL and HL Paper 1. This can be found in the ITGS Specimen Papers.

Exercise 9-4
Part 1
a)
Possible answers include:
- Jobs involving less teamwork and face to face contact with colleagues—since such meetings are more difficult to arrange with teleworking (for example, writing or translating documents, data entry, tele-sales work).
- Jobs that involve lots of travelling anyway—teleworking allows "wasted" travelling time to be utilised.

Award 1 mark for the description and 1 mark for the suitable expansion.

b)
Possible answers include:
- Jobs which involve direct supervision of personnel (for example, managers).
- Jobs that require significant onsite teamwork (such as construction).
- Jobs that require building.
- Jobs that require direct face-to-face contact with clients (for example, nursing).

Award 1 mark for the description and 1 mark for the suitable expansion.

Part 2
a & b)
Answers will vary greatly depending upon students' desired careers. Items to consider include:
- The amount of individual work involved versus the amount of working with colleagues.
- The nature of any work with colleagues—whether it requires face to face communication.
- Whether the work involves face-to-face contact with other people, such as customers or clients.
- Whether the work lends itself to being digitised.

Grade according to the 6 mark Explanation rubric on page 142.

c)
Possible answers include:
Benefits
- The possible benefits of being at home and spending time with family.
- The amount of money saved by not having to travel to work (transport costs, fuel costs).
- Time is saved by not having to travel to work.
- The individual's ability to work alone and find self-motivation.

Drawbacks
- The possibility of work invading on personal / social life—such as working outside normal office hours.
- The potential additional costs for electricity and equipment, and who will pay for them.
- The potential negative psychological impact of not having colleagues to speak and socialise with.

This exercise should be marked according to the generic ITGS extended response rubric for SL and HL Paper 1. This can be found in the ITGS Specimen Papers.

Exercise 9-5

This is a practical exercise to familiarise students with using word processing and desktop publishing software.

Exercise 9-6

Information: School policies (such as grading policies, uniform policies)

Explanation: These should be shared publicly on the Internet since they are of interest to both existing parents and students and potential future parents and students. They are also general and contain no personal information.

Information: Student grades

Explanation: Sharing these on the school intranet (which appropriate access restrictions) may be useful for heads of department and academic coordinators who want to assess overall student progress. Sharing the grades with parents via an extranet could also help improve school – parent communication.

Information: Students' personal details (medical details, contact information)

Explanation: Personal data such as this may be needed by various stakeholders around the school (administrators, teachers, pastoral care staff, school doctor / nurse) and so should be shared on the intranet (with appropriate security restrictions) but not with other stakeholders.

Information: Attendance information

Explanation: Staff around the school can make use of this information if shared via an intranet (for example, administrators can watch for students with low attendance). If this data is shared with parents via an extranet, it can improve school-parent communication and help reduce truancy in cases where parents have sent their children to school but they have not turned up.

Information: Details of school events

Explanation: This information should be shared with staff, students, and parents, so should at least be available on the school extranet. Depending on the exact content (for example, if there are no photos containing personal information such as names or classes), this might also be made public via the Internet.

Grade according to the 4 mark Explanation rubric on page 140, applying the rubric to a maximum of three answers.

Exercise 9-7

Students should make specific reference to the types of products mentioned in the question where possible, rather than giving general answers.

Possible answers include:
Advantages
- Shopping can be done at any time (no need to wait for shops to open).
- Access to a wider range of shops (not restricted to those in the local area).
- There is no need to travel to the shop – saving time and expenses (such as fuel).
- Often customizable products are available online that are not available in physical stores – for example, computers can be configured with a user's choice of RAM, hard disk, graphics card, and so on.
- Some products can be access instantly – for example, electronic versions of books, streaming videos, and computer software.
- Shoppers can see other customers' opinions – for example, product reviews.
- Targeted advertising can help recommend products to users.
- Products can be purchased for people in other countries from a store local to them, saving on shipping costs.

Do not allow: "Quicker" since products usually take longer to deliver than visiting a shop and purchasing in person.

Disadvantages
- Shopping can be slower because customers must wait for the item to be delivered in most cases (for example, clothes, computers, and groceries).
- It may be necessary to see some products in person before purchasing (for example, clothes or groceries).
- It can be difficult or expensive to return faulty goods.
- There may be security concerns about the use of credit cards online.
- There may be concern about the identity and integrity of a seller, especially on auction sites such as eBay or Amazon marketplace.
- Excessive online marketing (e.g. emails, popups,) can be annoying to users.

Grade according to the 6 mark Discuss rubric on page 142.

Exercise 9-9
Students should consider features including:
- Availability of product images (number, size and quality).
- Availability of a search function.
- Availability of search filters (for example, showing only footwear for women).
- Availability of user reviews.
- Availability of help options such as Frequently Asked Question pages (FAQs).
- Availability of contact information (email address, telephone number, etc.
- Location of navigation options
- Consistency of site layout.
- Additional options such as 'related products'.

Grade according to the 6 mark Explanation rubric on page 141.

Exercise 9-10
Students should demonstrate that they understand the need to logically group data. The sample diagram (page 133) groups by school section (primary, secondary, whole school), but there are other possible groupings, including by stakeholder (teachers, students, parents) and by curriculum (PYP, IGCSE, IB DP).

Grade according to the rubric on page 133.

Exercise 9-11
Example answer:

Web development software is used to create a website consisting of HTML pages. Styling data is added to the HTML using a CSS stylesheet. This helps keep content information (HTML) and formatting information (CSS) separate.

Data driven websites (dynamic web sites) are created by using ASP to connect to a database. Database records are then retrieved using SQL statements.

Exercise 9-12
Possible answers include:
Benefits
- The law would ensure a consistent, standard level of minimum accessibility—this improves equality of access for disabled users.
- As more and more information is available online, there is a greater risk of isolating disabled people if web sites are not accessible.
- Businesses and organisations can benefit—research

has shown that accessible web sites are easier to navigate not only for disabled users, but all users.
- Making web sites accessible opens up a relatively large portion of customers (some research suggests up to 20% of users have some form of disability).
- Some accessibility changes can increase search engine visibility (for example, ALT tags on images).
- Certain accessibility changes (such as text versions) may also be more usable for some non-disabled users (such as those with low bandwidth connections or text-only browsers).

Drawbacks
- Testing a web site for a wide range of accessibility features can be difficult, time consuming, and expensive—costs that the law forces upon the web master.
- Some businesses may benefit from making their web site accessible much less than others (for example, depending on their market demographic) - but the law will require all to implement the changes.
- Some accessibility changes (such as replacing interactive Flash animations text) may limit web site appearance / functionality.
- Some accessibility changes may require duplicating content (such as producing plain-text versions of interactive menus).
- Some web masters (e.g. those of amateur or hobby sites) may not have the knowledge or expertise to make a site accessible.

This exercise should be marked according to the generic ITGS extended response rubric for SL and HL Paper 1. This can be found in the ITGS Specimen Papers.

Exercise 9-13
Possible answers include:
- Web masters of amateur or hobby sites often rely on advertising to pay web hosting costs.
- Some users may never click on adverts anyway—thus blocking them makes little difference.
- Web masters may lose money from blocked adverts—advertisers pay for advert impressions (per thousand views), not just for clicks.
- Visitors may not wish to spend their time waiting for adverts to load before they can use a web page.
- Visitors who pay for their data by the megabyte are effectively paying to download and view the adverts—this is particularly bad for larger multimedia adverts.
- Most media (television, magazines) features advertisements which are automatically included with the

content—web sites function using a similar model.

- Some advertisement providers track users (which is considered a privacy violation by some)—blocking adverts can help prevent this.

Grade according to the 6 mark Explanation rubric on page 141.

Exercise 9-14

Students should look for information that may be determined by looking at a range of search queries, not just an individual search. It is expected that the conclusions made may not be 100% definite.

User 1's searches

Possible interpretations include:

- An owner of a Porsche 944
- Broken up with his girlfriend
- Likely a man
- Interested in golf
- Interested in reporting a crime

User 2's searches

Possible interpretations include:

- A woman
- A teacher
- Lives in Denver Colorado (or looking to move there)
- Separated (or about to be)
- Suffers depression
- Looking to adopt a child

Exercise 9-15

Students should consider interpretations of their search queries, not the literal meanings. For example, "Graduation dress" might literally imply that the user wants to find a graduation dress, but it might also imply "the user is female" and "the user is of school or college graduation age". Combined with other searches, more certainty could be added to these assertions.

Exercise 9-16

Possible answers include:

Benefits

- The mere presence of such scanners may deter potential terrorist attacks.
- These scanners may detect weapons and explosives that a metal detector cannot detect.
- The scanners are a relatively quick and efficient way to process large numbers of travellers.
- Alternatives (such as data-mining of passenger data)

raise similar privacy concerns.

- The images produced are 'outlines' rather than being photographic quality, and modern scanners can use a generic outline image of a person instead.
- It could be argued that human life / safety outweighs privacy concerns.

Drawbacks

- There are privacy concerns about the creation and storage of 'naked body' images of travellers. (Despite assurances that such images are not stored, several have already been leaked onto the Internet).
- There are concerns about the potential abuse of the scanners (for example, selecting celebrities, famous people, or particularly attractive people for a scan in order to view the resultant image).
- There are especial concerns about using these scanners to produce 'naked' images of children.
- There are health concerns over exposure to some types of scanners (backscatter x-ray machines).
- The use of such scanners treats everybody as a potential terrorist, even without suspicion.

This exercise should be marked according to the generic ITGS extended response rubric for SL and HL Paper 1. This can be found in the ITGS Specimen Papers.

Exercise 9-17

Data mining / profiling techniques

- Can be performed prior to the traveller arriving at the security area.
- Data mining techniques can identify patterns, trends, or anomalies which may be missed by human security checkers.
- Can potentially alert security staff to potential 'intent' (by analysing past connections / movements) even if the traveller is carrying no incriminating items or objects.
- The use of data matching and data mining techniques raises privacy concerns about the use of supposedly private data.
- Profiling passengers and giving different levels of security screening to different passengers may raise complaints about discrimination (e.g. racism, religious discrimination).

'Puffer' machines

- Enable chemical traces to be detected upon passengers' clothing.
- Removes the privacy concerns of body scanners.
- Analysis of any chemicals found on clothing is per-

formed by software—this removes the possibility of human error (such as misreading a scan result).

- Cannot detect hidden weapons / objects—only chemical traces that may be associated with explosives.

Physical pat-downs
- Vulnerable to human error (missing hidden objects / weapons).
- Slow to perform.
- Invasive for both the screen and the traveller being screened.

This exercise should be marked according to the generic ITGS extended response rubric for SL and HL Paper 1. This can be found in the ITGS Specimen Papers.

Exercise 9-18
Technologies students should consider here include:
- Self-parking cars
- Self-driving cars
- Collision avoidance systems
- Automatic road conditions warnings (ice, wet surface)
- Traffic alerts
- Satellite navigation systems
- Cars that dial emergency services in the event of an accident

Exercise 9-19
Hardware:
- Laptop, tablet, or other portable computer
- Smart phone
- External / portable hard drive

Software:
- Virtual Private Network (VPN) software
- Instant message ("chat") software

Exercise 9-20
Benefits for the customer
- More convenient – there is no need to stand in lines waiting to pay bills, saving time.
- Gives peace of mind - The payment process can be automated, meaning customers can be assured that bills are always paid on time (removing the chance of penalties for late payment).

Benefits for the utility company
- Reduces staff overheads, because fewer staff members need to deal with customers.
- The payment process can be automated – this saves the hassle of paying bills and ensures that they are always paid on time.
- Paperless bill payment can save money for the utility company (fewer bills printed, envelopes used, money spent on postage), as well as having environmental benefits which may improve the company's image.

Grade according to the 4 mark Explanation rubric on page 140. Award up to 4 marks for the benefits and 4 marks for the drawbacks.

Exercise 9-21
To improve bounce rate (lower is better)
- Make navigation options clearly visible—this avoids users leaving the site because they cannot find what they want.
- Divide navigation / menu options logically so users do not need to search through every option to find the required page.
- Make sure hyperlinks are distinguished (for example, by underlining and by colour) to ensure users can find them.
- Include a sitemap to help users quickly find what they need.
- Ensure page titles are accurate—so users do not arrive expecting content on a different topic, and leave when they cannot find it.
- Provide links to related content at the bottom of posts, so users can continue their search if the current page does not meet their requirements.
- If using advertisements, avoid making them very obtrusive—users may leave the site.
- Ensure the page works well in all browsers and on mobile devices – this avoids users leaving because the layout is poor or unusable on their device.
- Improve page loading times (for example, by removing very large graphics) to avoid frustrating users.

To improve Click Through Rate (CTR) (higher is better)
- HTML description metatags ('snippets') are used by search engines to display in their search listings—ensure they are clear and appealing to users.
- For advertisements, ensure they are targeted at the correct audience demographic (many ad companies allow this to be configured).
- Ensuring relevant keywords are included in the web

page (search engine optimisation) will improve search engine rank—which should improve CTR too.

- Use web traffic analysis to analyse campaigns and understand where users are clicking through to the web site (and where they aren't).
- Advertisement banners should be eye-catching but not off-putting (avoiding large amounts of animation or Flash).

To improve Conversion Rate (higher is better)

- Many of the answers for improving bounce rate also apply here.
- 'One-click buy' and similar functions can help encourage the user enter the buying process.
- 'Purchase' buttons should be prominently placed, and be above the page fold (i.e. visible without scrolling down).

Award 1 mark for the method identified and 1 mark for a description, up to 8 marks.

Exercise 9-22
Grade according to the rubric on page 134.

Exercise 9-23
a)
i) A piece of software or hardware [1 mark] that is used to keep a record of all keys pressed by the user. [1 mark]

ii)
Possible answers include:
- Staff details such as internal contact information—which is not for public use.
- Company policies (such as IT acceptable use policies) which are only for internal use.
- Client details such as contact details—which are only for project team members.
- Budget / financial details—which are only accessible by senior staff.

Award 1 mark for the method identified and 1 mark for a description, up to 4 marks.

b)
Possible answers include:
Provision: Restriction on the installation of unauthorised software.
Reason: To prevent possible infection by malware, and issues related to unlicensed copies of software.

Provision: No unauthorised access / hacking into other systems.
Reason: The company might be held legally responsible for actions performed using its networks and systems.

Provision: Restriction on access to social media sites
Reasons: Staff can waste time on such sites, reducing productivity. Company image can also be harmed by "unauthorised" social media posts. Bandwidth can be wasted on such sites.

Provision: Restriction on access to inappropriate sites including adult-content, obscene, offensive, or illegal material.
Reasons: Adult / obscene content can offend fellow workers, creating an uncomfortable working environment. The company might be held legally responsible for illegal content downloaded using its networks and systems.

Provision: No sharing passwords / accounts with other users. Users are responsible for all activity performed using their account.
Reason: Security can easily be breached in this way. Audit logs are less useful if multiple people share a single account.

Provision: No disclosure of confidential company information online.
Reasons: The company may be held legally accountable for breaches of data protection laws. The loss of confidential information can have a negative impact on the company / benefit competitors.

Provision: No posting of abusive or derogatory comments targeting about users, companies, or organisations.
Reason: The company might be held legally responsible for actions performed using its networks and systems (including cases of employee harassment).

Award 1 mark for the clause identified and 1 mark for an explanation, up to 6 marks.

c)
Possible answers include:
- The business owns the IT equipment and thus has the right to monitor its use.
- Monitoring software is used only on company-owned equipment to ensure it is used for work purposes.
- Monitoring processes are documented in company policies—it is not done without the employees' knowledge.

- Monitoring software helps provide evidence in case of alleged misconduct (avoids false accusations).
- Monitoring software improves employee efficiency, which benefits all workers.
- Monitoring software helps the efficiency of the IT systems / networks (for example, by identifying bandwidth hogs, sources of malware, etc.).
- Monitoring software can be used to assess employee performance (good performance as well as bad).
- Monitoring software may be legally required in some industries / countries.
- The results of monitoring might only be checked if an allegation or problem arises, rather than being continuously or routinely monitored.

This exercise should be marked according to the generic ITGS extended response rubric for SL and HL Paper 1. This can be found in the ITGS Specimen Papers.

Exercise 9-24

a)

i)

Possible answers include:
- Users may be tricked into revealing the card details (phishing scam).
- Card details may be secretly copied during the payment process (e.g. by restaurant waiter).
- 'Skimming' devices surreptitiously attached to Automatic Teller Machines (ATMs) may copy card details during a normal transaction.
- Malware / spyware may log the user's keystrokes (including card details) during an online transaction.
- The card may be physically stolen and used.

Do not allow: card number / details may be guessed or made up.

ii)

Possible answers include:
- Transaction / account history—the ability to view all withdrawals and deposits in a specified time period.
- Pay bills—paying the utility provider directly by means of special bank-utility company relationship.
- Transfer money—electronic transfer of money to another bank account.
- Report fraud—email or telephone contact to report fraud such as stolen cards, suspicious transactions, or phishing emails.
- Offers / other products—ability to buy other products and services the bank offers.

- Make an appointment—easy online appointments with financial advisors or bank managers.
- Security settings—ability to change / request new security settings (e.g. for telephone banking, online banking, ATM PIN).
- Security help and advice—information on best practises for secure online transactions.

Award 1 mark for the method identified and 1 mark for a description, up to 4 marks.

b)

Possible answers include:
- Encryption between the web server and the user (SSL / TLS / https) to ensure that the transactions cannot be read by other, unauthorised users.
- Digital certificates (Extended Validation SSL) to authenticate the bank to the user / assure the user that the web site to which they connect is genuine.
- Two factor authentication such as a password and a security token to improve security and prevent unauthorised access to a user's account.
- IP address / location logging—enabling it to alert users if a login from an unknown device or location occurs.
- Login notification—sending an email or text message (SMS) to a user when they log into their account (perhaps only when using a new device or from a new location) to confirm the login was authorised.
- Requiring a users to regularly change their password—reducing problems if it is compromised.
- Enforcing password requirements (such as minimum length, use of numbers, symbols, and letters) to ensure users avoid weak passwords.
- Using a virtual keyboard for login rather than have the user type their username and password—makes it difficult for key loggers to log passwords.

Grade according to the 6 mark Explanation rubric on page 141.

c)

Possible answers include:

Benefits for banks
- Fewer staff will need to be employed to serve customers at branches.
- Fewer branches may be needed; this results in cost savings.

Benefits for customers
- Bank services can be accessed 24 hours a day, from any location with an Internet connected device.
- There is no need to wait in line to be served.

- Transactions may be processed immediately, rather than at the end of the day as they might be via an ATM or clerk.

Drawbacks for banks
- Banks lose large amounts of money due to online fraud (often they absorb their customers' losses).
- Extra staff may be needed to man telephone / email helplines or customer support services.

Drawbacks for customers
- Security is a major concern—and it can take months or even years to recover from crimes such as identity theft.
- There is a less personal service—some customers may prefer banking in person.
- Some services which must still be done in person may now be harder because the bank has fewer branches and staff.

This exercise should be marked according to the generic ITGS extended response rubric for SL and HL Paper 1. This can be found in the ITGS Specimen Papers.

Exercise 9-25
a)
i)
A web site whose content is stored in a database [1 mark] and fetched dynamically when the page is displayed. [1 mark]

ii)
Possible answers include:
- Use ALT tags on images—a description of an image can be read by a screen reader better than a URL (for partially sighted or blind users).
- Navigation options should be placed at the top or the left—this means screen readers read the navigation options before the page content (for partially sighted or blind users).
- Avoid certain colour schemes such as red-green—these colours are often indiscernible to colour blind users.
- Use Cascading Style Sheets (CSS) for site layout—this makes it easier for an accessibility-aware web browser to change the page's colour schemes, font size, and so on.

Award 1 mark for the method identified and 1 mark for a description, up to 4 marks.

b)
Possible answers include:
- Key words density—keywords that appear more frequently may be ranked higher (to an extent).
- Position of words in a page—words in page titles or headers may be considered more important.
- Number of incoming links—sites with more links to them may be ranked higher.
- Quality of incoming links—links from large and popular sites are considered as important 'recommendations'.
- Age of content—newer content may be ranked higher than older content.
- Number of reciprocal links—a set of sites which merely link to each other may be punished for 'link exchanging'.

Award 1 mark for the method identified and 1 mark for an explanation.

c)
Possible answers include:
Benefits of third party payment
- Especially for small businesses, a third party provider (such as PayPal) may be considered a more trustworthy brand.
- Third party providers specialise in online payment—they are likely to have established, efficient, and secure systems for purchasing.

Drawbacks of third party payment
- The third party provider will likely charge a fee or commission.
- Some customers may be put off by being redirected to a third party during the purchasing process.
- It is harder to integrate the payment process into the business' web site if the user must be redirected to another site.
- The refund process may be more complicated.
- If there is a problem, customers must rely on the payment provider's customer support.

Benefits of direct card handling
- Customers may prefer to deal directly with the business rather than a third party.
- The business is not dependent on another company (and the potential reliability problems they may have).

Drawbacks of direct processing
- The business must set up their own web server to deal with payments, including security issues. This

takes significant expertise.
- Initial equipment and setup costs may be high.
- Staff may need training to meet legal requirements— for example, in terms of data protection policies.

This exercise should be marked according to the generic ITGS extended response rubric for SL and HL Paper 1. This can be found in the ITGS Specimen Papers.

Exercise 9-26
a)
i) The checkout where customers pay for goods [1 mark] which communicates with a centralised database to fetch / update stock details [1 mark].

b)
ii)
- The product's barcode is scanned with a barcode scanner.
- The barcode number is sent to a centralised database
- The barcode number is matched against a table of products / the product's record is retrieved.
- The relevant fields (product name, price) are sent back to the POS.
- The 'stock' field is reduced by 1.
- The price of the product is added to the total, and the item is added to the bill.

Award 1 mark per step, up to 4 marks

c)
Possible answers include:
- Points are accumulated at every use which may earn discounts.
- Customers may have a feeling of membership or being a 'preferred customer'.
- Customers with loyalty cards may get access to special benefits (for example, airline frequent flyer cards gain access to special lounges).
- Customers can get special offers and advertisements aimed particularly at their interests or the products they frequently buy.

Grade according to the 6 mark Explanation rubric on page 141.

Award 1 mark for the method identified and 1 mark for an explanation, up to 6 marks.

c)
Benefits of RFID
- Goods leaving / entering warehouses can be scanned very accurately and very quickly (compared to barcodes).
- RFID tags can be read from a distant—meaning staff can scan shelves for extremely quick stock-taking procedures.
- Individual products can be tracked, as every RFID tag is unique.
- Supermarkets can implement new technologies such as self-checkout, contactless payment, and smart shopping trolleys more efficiently than with barcodes.
- RFID tags can be used to detect hidden items that customers may be attempting to steal.
- RFID tags in products, shelves, and customer loyalty cards enable supermarkets to gain unprecedented data about not only purchasing habits, but shopping and browsing habits.

Concerns over RFID
- Privacy concerns—in-shelf RFID readers can track products (and thus customers) around a supermarket, building a profile of customer movements.
- There are some concerns that RFID tags in products could be used to track customers outside of the store.
- There are concerns that customer loyalty cards could be RFID-tagged—enabling supermarkets to potentially track the paths customers take around their stores.
- RFID tags are very small and thus can be easily concealed.

This exercise should be marked according to the generic ITGS extended response rubric for SL and HL Paper 1. This can be found in the ITGS Specimen Papers.

Education

Chapter 10 Solutions

Exercise 10-1
Possible answers include:

- Filtering software can be installed on all computers – this uses a variety of techniques (keyword filtering, blacklists) to block access to some inappropriate material. *(Do not allow: "All inappropriate material")*
- Monitoring software can be installed on all computers – this allows the teacher or system administrators to view a user's activities, including web pages visitors and in some cases, a copy of the user's screen.
- Students can be educated about acceptable use – this involves teaching students about appropriate and inappropriate online content and behaviour, and making sure they are aware of the school's acceptable use policy.
- Classroom configuration can be altered to make computer screens visible and discourage inappropriate browsing– for example, putting the teacher's desk behind students or arranging computers around the edge of a room.

Award 1 mark for the method identified and 1 mark for a description, up to 6 marks.

Exercise 10-2
Possible answers include:

Advantages:
- Skills such as research and source assessment can be tested—which cannot be easily done in traditional exams.
- Skills such as research and source assessment are 'real life' skills and often required in the workplace—the exams may better prepare students for the workplace.

Problems and limitations:
- Reliability issues related to hardware, software, and networking will need to be resolved to prevent students losing work before submission.
- Concerns relating to students cheating (accessing pre-prepared material or communicating with third parties) will need to be solved.
- Concerns relating to possible plagiarism by students must be addressed.
- There are equality of access issues relating to students with disabilities, which may need additional time or specific computer configurations (for example, accessibility settings turned on).

This exercise should be marked according to the generic ITGS extended response rubric for SL and HL Paper 1. This can be found in the ITGS Specimen Papers.

Exercise 10-3
Possible answers include:

- Teachers may believe students will be distracted from learning—for example on non-educational sites such as social networks.
- There may be concerns that students will cheat in assignments—for example, plagiarising work from the Internet instead of completing it themselves.
- There may be concerns regarding students accessing inappropriate material during lesson time (for example, pornography) - this could reflect badly on the teacher and the school (and leave them open to legal issues).
- The teacher may lack training in the use of the hardware and software—this may make them reluctant to use the equipment in case students encounter problems that they cannot fix.
- The teacher may lack training in using technology for educational purposes—the teacher may not know what functions and features the equipment has, and how it can be used to improve their lessons.
- The teacher may be concerned that time will be wasted fixing problems—for example, if students are very young or inexperienced, Internet connectivity is poor, or IT support teams are not available.

Award 1 mark for the method identified and 1 mark for an explanation, up to 8 marks.

Exercise 10-4

- Tracking software / hardware can be installed on computers – this means that if the computer is stolen and later connected to the internet, it should be possible to locate it.
- Physical security on buildings such as door locks or key codes – these measures prevent access to computers outside of permitted times, reducing the chance of theft.
- Physical laptop security, including desk chains (Kensington locks) and secure storage cabinets – these measures prevent physical access to computers and reduce the chance of theft.
- Secure sign-in / sign-out system – each student's identity can be recorded when they borrow a school laptop. This somewhat reduces the chance of theft by making it easier to track the movement of the laptop.

- Security cameras can be installed in computer laboratories and around the school. These can deter would-be thieves who fear they may be caught on camera.
- Students can be educated about secure practices. This reduces the chances of opportunist theft caused by students leaving laptops unattended or unsecured in bags or corridors.

Award 1 mark for the method identified and 1 mark for an explanation, up to 6 marks.

Exercise 10-5
Possible answers include:

Reasons for the school to pay

- Schools can buy the same hardware and software for all students—this potentially reduces problems such as hardware, software, and file incompatibility.
- Ensuring all students have the same equipment means some students are not disadvantaged compared to others (for example, if they had laptops with greater capabilities).
- Poorer families may not be able to afford to buy equipment for their children—this could put them at a serious disadvantage if the school does not provide equipment.
- Schools have greater rights over the laptop—for example, the right to install filtering and monitoring software on them. Typically they could not do this on a student-owned machine.
- IT support may be easier if the technicians are dealing with a known range of hardware and software.

Reasons for parents to pay

- Students may be more responsible with equipment if they (or their parents) paid for it—this may ensure it lasts longer.
- Costs for the school could be lower—in terms of initial investment, maintenance and repair costs, software licences, and insurance.
- Students taking laptops home becomes easier if they own them.

This exercise should be marked according to the generic ITGS extended response rubric for SL and HL Paper 1. This can be found in the ITGS Specimen Papers.

Exercise 10-6
Grade according to the rubric on page 135.

Exercise 10-7
Possible answers include:

- Effective implementation requires teachers to be trained in the use of common hardware, software and networking technologies.
- Effective implementation requires professional development for teachers so they are aware of the benefits of IT in the classroom.
- The success of technology in the classroom depends greatly on supporting IT infrastructure (such as reliable and high bandwidth Internet connectivity, or electrical sockets for charging laptops).
- Effective implementation requires quality IT support to help teachers and students quickly resolve any problems.
- Policies are required to ensure the effective use of technology—for example Acceptable Use Policies (AUP) which state appropriate and inappropriate behaviour.

This exercise should be marked according to the generic ITGS extended response rubric for SL and HL Paper 1. This can be found in the ITGS Specimen Papers.

Exercise 10-8
a)

i) Open content is material that can be copied (distributed) for free [1 mark] and can be modified by anyone [1 mark].

ii)
Possible answers include:

- E-book readers or tablets—these may be needed if the school plans to implement large scale use of electronic books.
- Laptops (perhaps ruggedized versions)—to serve as a general mobile computing platform for content creation.
- Wireless routers—may be needed to ensure all areas of the school campus have fast access to Internet based resources.
- Servers—may be required to hold copies of shared data on the school's Local Area Network (LAN).
- Peripheral devices such as printers that can be shared on the network for all users.

Award 1 mark for the method identified and 1 mark for a description, up to 4 marks.

b)

Possible answers include:

- Ensuring the physical security of the laptops—to prevent theft or loss
- Hardware protection—to prevent accidental damage to the laptops (e.g. through spillages, drops, etc.).
- Monitoring of students' Internet activities—to prevent behaviour such as cyber-bullying or accessing inappropriate content online.
- Internet filtering of undesirable content—this may be requested by parents and teachers, and may be a legal requirement.
- Online safety training—students and teachers will need educating about appropriate and inappropriate online activities and potential dangers such as revealing too much personal information online.

Grade according to the 6 mark Explanation rubric on page 141.

c)

Possible answers include:

Arguments in favour of open textbooks

- Costs are very low—cheaper than both paper textbooks and e-books.
- Textbooks can be given to all students and staff without any increase in costs.
- Content may be updated more frequently than both paper books and commercial e-books.
- Staff members can update the books themselves or adapt them to their course.
- Books can be given to students without the need to recollect them at the end of the year.
- Content can still be downloaded and printed if staff or students prefer paper books.

Arguments against open textbooks

- Frequent updates to open content can make teaching harder as students may have different book versions and teaching materials may need updating.
- Staff may be unlikely to contribute to open content if the licence requires them to give their work away for free too.
- Open textbooks may not be written by experienced academic authors—this could affect the accuracy of the content.
- Open textbooks may not meet educational standards / outcomes set down to national or local education authorities.
- Truly open content can be vandalised (deliberately incorrect edits can be made).
- Internet connectivity may be required to access the books.

- Reader devices (tablets, e-book readers, or laptops) will be needed for every student.
- Books may be inaccessible to students at home if they do not have access to a laptop, e-book reader, or the Internet.

This exercise should be marked according to the generic ITGS extended response rubric for SL and HL Paper 1. This can be found in the ITGS Specimen Papers.

Exercise 10-9

a)

i)

Virtual Learning Environment—a shared online site [1 mark] where teachers and students can upload resources, assignments, and other learning material related to a specific course or topic [1 mark].

ii)

Possible answers include:

- Allowing trends in student data to be viewed—for example, viewing grades from previous terms and years to see progress (or lack of).
- Storing essential information that may be needed for support staff—such as medical conditions, required medications, or similar.
- Improving contact with home—by storing contact details for parents and guardians and storing details of past contacts.
- Automatically alerting administrators if a student is not in class, or if absence has reached a particular level.
- Allowing administrators to immediately locate a student—by storing their timetable, teacher allocation, and room allocation.

Award 1 mark for the method identified and 1 mark for a description, up to 4 marks.

b)

Possible answers include:

- Educating students about plagiarism, what constitutes plagiarism, and how to correctly cite sources—this can address "accidental plagiarism" problems.
- Teachers can compare submitted work with students' previous work—this allows them to become familiar with a student's style and makes it easier to notice changes that may indicate third-party work has been included.
- Online plagiarism checking services can be used—teachers upload student work to the service, which

then compares it with web pages and work submitted by other students.

- Teachers can design assignments in such a way to discourage plagiarism—for example, by posing questions that require students' opinions rather than simply regurgitating facts.

Grade according to the 6 mark Explanation rubric on page 141.

c)
Possible answers include:
In favour of interactive whiteboards:
- Younger children in particular can find interactive whiteboards fun and engaging.
- Students can be involved with demonstrating and explaining tasks and answers in front of the class.
- The whiteboard offers a more natural method of interaction than the traditional computer—this may be particularly useful for younger children.
- Content from the whiteboard can easily be distributed to students after class via email.

In favour of other uses:
- In large classes, interactive whiteboards may discourage interaction (since only one child can use it at once).
- Resources for interactive whiteboards can be difficult to produce and expensive to purchase.
- Whiteboards can be easily damaged.
- For the same expenditure, students may get more benefits from devices, such as laptops.

This exercise should be marked according to the generic ITGS extended response rubric for SL and HL Paper 1. This can be found in the ITGS Specimen Papers.

Exercise 10-10
a)
i)
Blended learning involves using traditional face-to-face learning methods [1 mark] in conjunction with e-learning technologies [1 mark].

ii)
Possible answers include:
- Laptop / device with Internet access—needed to access online resources.
- Speakers—required to listen to any multimedia resources that may be posted.
- Broadband Internet connection—may be needed if large amounts of multimedia is used.

Award 1 mark for the method identified and 1 mark for a description, up to 4 marks.

b)
Possible answers include:
- Class wikis—can be used as a collaborative class space to save work and useful resources.
- Blogs—can be used by students as individual journals or records of work, accessible from home as well as school, and by parents.
- Social bookmarking tools—can be used to maintain lists of useful classroom resources, divided by topic.
- Social networks—can be used to communicate and cooperate with students in other schools, for collaborative projects.
- Virtual Learning Environment (VLE) - used as a central repository for class assignments and resources, managed by the teacher.

Grade according to the 6 mark Explanation rubric on page 141.

c)
Possible answers include:
Benefits
- Students can gain access to a wide range of resources on the Internet—much more information is available to them than before.
- Students are able to learn independently, using online resources.

Drawbacks
- Laptop donation programmes can be plagued by maintenance and repair problems.
- Theft of the laptops can be a significant issue.
- Students are often given little or no training on how to use the laptops.
- The laptops (and access to the Internet) may result in a culture shift—the 'Westernization' of children.

This exercise should be marked according to the generic ITGS extended response rubric for SL and HL Paper 1. This can be found in the ITGS Specimen Papers.

Exercise 10-11
Possible answers include:
- There may be concerns that too much time will be wasted setting up laptops and fixing problems, which distracts from learning.
- There may be concerns that the cost of such programs (including on-going costs) will be too high.
- There may be concerns that students could access

inappropriate material online.

- There may be concerns that students may engage in activities such as cyber-bullying.
- There may be concerns for the online safety of students—for example giving away too much personal information online.
- There may be concerns about the health of students if they spend many hours each day using a computer.
- Parents and school administrators may lack first-hand experience of technology—they may rely on the media for their information.
- Parents and school administrators may lack training or understanding of the problems (and solutions) related to using technology in school.
- Parents and administrators may believe there is little benefit to using laptops compared to traditional teaching and learning methods.
- Parents and administrators may see laptops merely as electronic versions of traditional teaching and learning methods—for example, a word processor instead of a notebook, a web page instead of a text-book—rather than see the new opportunities and tools that are available.

This exercise should be marked according to the generic ITGS extended response rubric for SL and HL Paper 1. This can be found in the ITGS Specimen Papers.

Chapter 11
Environment

Chapter 11 Solutions

Exercise 11-1

This exercise is intended as a quick class or pair discussion to introduce the Environment topic. Items students might want to consider include:

Arguments that IT is a 'clean industry'
- Technologies such as teleworking and video-conferencing can reduce the need to travel (which reduces pollution).
- Online shopping reduces the need to travel to shops (which reduces pollution).
- Technologies such as e-books reduce paper use.
- Online documents and email reduce paper use.

Arguments that IT is not a 'clean industry'
- Large amounts of IT equipment are disposed of each year (often unsafely).
- IT equipment often contains large amounts of harmful chemicals.
- IT manufacture consumes huge amounts of raw material resources.
- IT equipment can use large amounts of electricity (often on devices that could be switched off).

Exercise 11-2

Students should consider the various electronic items they have owned and how they disposed of them. This can be used to start a discussion about the speed at which we upgrade our electronic devices, and about appropriate disposal methods. In my experience this exercise is eye-opening for students, as their list of devices grows in front of them.

It is worth reminding students to consider devices such as chargers, printers (and ink cartridges), digital cameras, and other devices they may forget.

Exercise 11-3

a)
i)
An Operating System is a piece of software [1 mark] which manages the computer's hardware, its resources, and the application programs it runs. [1 mark]

ii)
Possible answers include:
- Toxic chemicals in discarded equipment may leach into water supplies over time (for example, when it rains). This can poison people consuming the water.
- Toxic chemicals in discarded equipment may leach into the soil over time (for example, when it rains). This can poison people consuming food grown in the soil.
- Burning discarded equipment can produce toxic gasses. These can poison the people burning the equipment and those in the vicinity.
- People can attempt to recover valuable elements (such as gold) from the equipment by using toxic chemicals such as sulphuric acid. This can produce fumes which have serious health effects on the recycler.

Award 1 mark for the method identified and 1 mark for a description, up to 4 marks.

b)
Possible answers include:
- Users might be concerned that their personal data may be left on the hard drive—this could be later recovered and used by criminal (for example, for identity theft).
- Users might be concerned that the company accepting that computer does not donate it to a worthwhile cause but simply sends it for unsafe recycling, causing environmental impacts. This problem is exacerbated by the lack of regulation of such companies.

Grade according to the 6 mark Explanation rubric on page 141.

c)
Possible answers include:
Reducing harmful chemicals in equipment
- Requires manufacturers to invest in new methods and processes that use less harmful chemicals.
- Less harmful chemicals may be more expensive—this cost could be pushed to consumers.
- Reduction of harmful chemicals could be enforced relatively easily by law.
- Could remove the most harmful chemicals from equipment.
- Equipment will still need disposal at its end of life.

Reusing equipment
- A lot of IT is still fully functional and quite modern when it is discarded (especially equipment from large companies).
- Users and organisations may be reluctant to donate equipment for fear it contains personal data that could be misused later.

- Equipment will still need to be safely disposed at its end of life—and this may be more difficult, depending upon where the hardware has been donated.
- Organisations may be reluctant to accept donated equipment if they do not have the facilities to correctly dispose of it later.

Recycling equipment
- IT equipment often contains valuable raw materials (such as gold) that recyclers may be interested in recovering.
- Recycling IT is a difficult process which requires a great deal of effort and energy for relatively small rewards.

This exercise should be marked according to the generic ITGS extended response rubric for SL and HL Paper 1. This can be found in the ITGS Specimen Papers.

Exercise 11-4
Linked to exercise 11-2, this exercise can be used to start a discussion about how the manufacturers of students' equipment fare, and what changes students might make to their buying habits in the future.

Exercise 11-5
Possible answers include:
- Automatically blurring of vehicle licence plates / number plates (for example, all such images in Google Street View are automatically blurred). This provides some level of privacy but users may still be identified.
- Automatic blurring of faces (for example, all faces in Google Street View are automatically blurred). This provides some level of privacy but vehicles and users may still be identified.
- Removal requests—mapping providers can provide facilities for users to request removal of images (such as images of their house).
- Mapping companies can use older data (for example, many months or even several years old) to mitigate the privacy concerns somewhat.

Students should evaluate the effectiveness of these solutions.

This exercise should be marked according to the generic ITGS extended response rubric for SL and HL Paper 1. This can be found in the ITGS Specimen Papers.

Exercise 11-6
a)

i)

Possible answers include:
- Arsenic
- Beryllium
- BFR (Brominated Flame Retardants)
- Cadmium
- Hexavalent Chromium
- Lead
- Mercury
- PVC (Polyvinyl Chloride)

ii)
- Erasing the hard disk with special wiping software—this overwrites every sector of the disk with random data.
- Physical destruction of the disk, such as drilling holes in it—this makes the disk unusable.

Award 1 mark for the method identified and 1 mark for a description, up to 4 marks.

Do not allow: 'deleting files' or 'formatting the disk'.

b)
Possible answers include:
- Manufacturers could reduce the harmful chemicals in their products. This would mean there are fewer harmful chemicals in equipment that could potentially leach into the water or ground if they are incorrectly discarded.
- Manufacturers could implement take-back schemes for old equipment. This could reduce discarded IT equipment, enable the recovery of valuable materials, and ensure safe recycling.
- Governments could create and enforce laws governing the disposal of IT equipment or the chemicals equipment contains. Laws can be more effective than simple voluntary measures implemented by other stakeholders.
- Users could ensure that they dispose of their old IT equipment responsibly. This could reduce the problem of e-waste related water and ground pollution.
- Users could buy only from manufacturers with clear and responsible environment policies. This could encourage or even force other manufacturers to adopt similar policies.

Grade according to the 6 mark Discuss rubric on page 142.

c)

Possible answers include:

Manufacturers

- Manufacturers create these devices and choose to use harmful chemicals—indicating they have at least some responsibility.
- They profit from the sale of these devices so should pay for their clean-up—indicating they have at least some responsibility.
- They create the problem by continually releasing new products (driving the upgrade-cycle)—indicating they have at least some responsibility.
- They could benefit by accepting back their own products and reusing the components or materials.
- They could use their equipment take-back schemes to promote a "green image" for their business.

Customers

- Benefit from these devices, so have responsibility for their safe disposal.
- Have safe disposal options available to them—but may need educating about their availability.
- Could "vote with their wallet" by only buying from manufacturers with environmentally-friendly policies.
- Are the driving force for upgrades and new models.

Other stakeholders

- Governments have a responsibility to provide / regulate safe recycling facilities.
- Governments have a responsibility to prevent e-waste exports (in MEDCs) and e-waste imports (in LEDCs).
- Can enforce safe recycling or the use of less harmful chemicals by making it a legal requirement.

This exercise should be marked according to the generic ITGS extended response rubric for SL and HL Paper 1. This can be found in the ITGS Specimen Papers.

Exercise 11-7

a)

i)

The use of a satellite with sensors [1 mark] to collect data about the environment [1 mark], typically for use in mapping applications.

ii)

Possible answers include:

Advantages

- Data can be collected about objects that are far beyond the reach of physical measurement—such as the surfaces of other planets.
- Data can be collected from very large areas (such as a planet's surface) relatively quickly.
- Many types of sensor can 'see through' weather conditions that would obscure photographs (such as cloud).

Award 1 mark for the disadvantage identified and 1 mark for a description, up to 2 marks.

Disadvantages

- The collected data is not a visual image—it must first be interpreted / processed to produce one.
- Equipment setup can be extremely expensive (it requires a satellite).

Award 1 mark for the advantage identified and 1 mark for a description, up to 2 marks.

b)

Possible answers include:

- Users might be concerned that their personal data may be left on the hard drive—this could be later recovered and used by criminal (for example, for identity theft).
- Users might be concerned that the company accepting that computer does not donate it to a worthwhile cause but simply sends it for unsafe recycling, causing environmental impacts. This problem is exacerbated by the lack of regulation of such companies.

Grade according to the 6 mark Explanation rubric on page 141.

c)

Possible answers include:

Benefits

- Users gain access to a wealth of mapping data in a more convenient form than paper maps.
- Users can benefit from additional features such as route finding, which are not available in paper maps.
- Businesses can use mapping systems to promote themselves and help customers find them (for example, in searches).
- Online mapping can be much more up-to-date than printed maps or atlases.
- The data provided by most online mapping systems is free—unlike paper based maps and atlases.

Concerns

- Privacy concerns—users may be concerned that satellite imagery invades otherwise private areas of their property—such as gardens.
- Safety concerns—people may be concerned that such imagery facilitates theft by allowing thieves to virtually search for attractive targets.
- National security—governments may be concerned that images of sensitive sites—such as military bases, nuclear power stations, and airports—may be used by terrorists to plan attacks.
- Many concerns can be alleviated through simple techniques such as blurring parts of the images.

This exercise should be marked according to the generic ITGS extended response rubric for SL and HL Paper 1. This can be found in the ITGS Specimen Papers.

Chapter 12
Health

Chapter 12 Solutions

Exercise 12-1
Possible answers include:
- Predictions could be used to decide how aggressively to treat a patient.
- Predictions could be used to predict availability of hospital resources (e.g. beds).
- Predictions could be used to provide advice and guidance to relatives.
- The reliability / accuracy of the predictions may be a concern.
- There may be concerns about relying on a machine for advice rather than human expertise.

Grade according to the 6 mark Explanation rubric on page 141.

Exercise 12-2
Possible answers include:
- Expert systems present a range of recommendations, often ranked or graded with a 'confidence interval' - they do not provide guarantees. Doctors need training to be aware of this.
- The expert system's recommendations may take into account situations or conditions (such as adverse drug interactions) that the doctor might not otherwise identify—this could improve a patient's outcome.
- There is a danger that the doctor may misinterpret the output from the expert system—this could lead to administration of incorrect medication or other treatment.
- Doctors can make mistakes (such as recommending incorrect treatment) just as computer systems can make incorrect recommendations
- Often the legal responsibility for a mistake is with the doctor—this might make them less willing to trust the IT system
- Doctors are often legally required to manually check recommendations made by IT systems.

This exercise should be marked according to the generic ITGS extended response rubric for SL and HL Paper 1. This can be found in the ITGS Specimen Papers.

Exercise 12-3
Issue: The patient may have reservations about the accuracy of the system.
Explanation: These concerns could make the patient reluc-
tant to trust a doctor who uses the system, even if these fears are not well-founded, leading to a loss of patient confidence.

Issue: Reliability of the system software and rules.
Explanation: Errors made during the programming of the system could lead to incorrect diagnoses, which could potentially be harmful and leave the doctor open to legal action.

Issue: Integrity: whether the system is up to date.
Explanation: Even if the data in the expert system is correct, inaccurate diagnoses may be made if the knowledge base is not updated to reflect the latest medical understanding (for example, the latest drugs or details of adverse drug interactions). This could have health impacts for the patient and legal ramifications for the doctor.

Issue: The patient may lose faith in the doctor.
Explanation: The patient may believe that the doctor is not an expert in their field and is merely following the advice of a computer program. The patient may see no reason to visit a doctor when they could find similar advice themselves (online for example).

Award 1 mark for identifying the issue and 1 mark for the explanation, up to 8 marks.

Exercise 12-4
Possible answers include:
- Mobile workers often use portable devices such as laptops or tablets. These often lack ergonomic features – for example, separate screens and keyboards that can be adjusted to suit the user.
- Mobile workers work in a variety of environments, including while on the move. These environments often lack ergonomic fixtures – for example, chairs with adjustable heights and supportive backs, foot rests, and desks of the appropriate height.
- Mobile workers have to carry their equipment with them. They may not have space to carry additional items such as separate keyboards, mice, or wrist supports.

Grade according to the 6 mark Explanation rubric on page 141.

Exercise 12-5
Grade according to the rubric on page 136.

Exercise 12-6

a)

Hardware

- Microphone so the patient can hear the doctor and vice versa.
- Video camera to allow the doctor to see the patient and their symptoms (possibly vice versa too).
- A high bandwidth (broadband) connection to allow the sending of real time video data.

Software

- Virtual Private Network (VPN) software to ensure security of the connection.
- Video conferencing software if the consultation is video or audio based.
- Instant messaging ("chat") software if the consultation is text based.

b)

Hardware

- Sensors that measure key aspects of the patient's health (for example, heart rate, breathing rate).
- Analog to digital converter (ADC) to convert the readings from the sensors into digital form.
- Internet connection to transmit the data back to the doctor.
- Video camera to allow the remote doctors to see the patient (as in Project Gerhome).

Software

- Monitoring software that automatically transmits data over a network.
- Virtual Private Network (VPN) software to ensure security of the connection.

c)

Hardware

- A "robotic device" with arms and medical tools which operates on the patient, controlled by the remote doctor.
- Specialised input devices used by the remote doctor to control the robotic device.
- Video cameras to allow the doctor to see the patient.
- Sensors to measure key aspects of the patient's health (for example, heart rate, breathing, blood pressure).
- A high bandwidth network connection to transmit video images and doctor's inputs.

Software

- Monitoring software to transmit the patient's vital signs to the doctor.
- Software in the "robot" to smooth the doctor's inputs

and transmits them to the robotic output devices.

- Virtual Private Network (VPN) software to ensure security of the connection.

Exercise 12-7

Possible answers include:

Benefits

- Being able to locate a patient immediately reduces the health and safety risks to the patient.
- The tracking systems could be combined with an alert system to notify family members if a patient leaves a certain area—this could further help reduce safety risks to the patient.
- Families members and carers may have increased peace of mind, knowing that they will be able to locate the patient.
- The patient gains some degree of independence—they do not need to be constantly accompanied by carers (depending on the extent of their illness).

Drawbacks

- The system could create a false sense of security—although it helps locate patients, it does not prevent accidents (such as wandering into busy roads or dangerous areas).
- There may be privacy concerns related to tracking a person—especially if the tracking happens 24 hours a day.
- There may be concerns that the tracking company sells personal data about the patient and their families—for example, to advertisers of related medical products and services.
- There could be an over-reliance on the system, isolating the patient—carers might not give patients the time and attention they need.

This exercise should be marked according to the generic ITGS extended response rubric for SL and HL Paper 1. This can be found in the ITGS Specimen Papers.

Exercise 12-8

Possible answers include:

- User access levels must be implemented (for example, pharmacies can only read prescription data but not diagnoses; doctors can only read and write data for their own patients). This ensures that only authorised users can access data, reducing data theft and privacy problems.
- Strong authentication mechanisms such as strong passwords or biometrics should be implemented on

user accounts. This reduces the chances of unauthorised users accessing accounts by guessing passwords.

- Security policies should be created and shared with staff. This ensures that everybody knows their responsibilities regarding security and follows best practice.
- Physical security must be implemented (such as locks on rooms and physical securing of machines). This reduces the chance of a computer or hard drive being stolen, along with the data on it.
- All data must be encrypted. This prevents unauthorised access to the data should a computer or hard drive be stolen.

Award 1 mark for the precaution identified and 1 mark for a description, up to 6 marks.

Exercise 12-9
Possible answers include:

- Reliability and speed of network connection — the bandwidth must be sufficiently high and the latency sufficiently low to enable real time communication between the remote doctor and the robotic surgery system. Any lag in feedback could result in surgical errors being made.
- Failover / standby systems such as backup power are needed in both locations — this is to prevent harm to the patient if there is an equipment failure at either location.
- Standby staff are needed in the surgery room — they are essential to assist the remote doctor and to take care of any potential problems that cannot be fixed by the robotic surgery system.
- The network must be secure from interference and unauthorised access — in the worst case scenarios, unauthorised access to the network connection could result in disabling or even controlling the connection between doctor and patient.
- Patients may be reluctant to use the system — they may (rightly or wrongly) fear equipment or network failure, or "out of control robots". These concerns must be solved before the system can be widely implemented.

This exercise should be marked according to the generic ITGS extended response rubric for SL and HL Paper 1. This can be found in the ITGS Specimen Papers.

Exercise 12-10
Possible answers include:
Technical solutions

- Software can be used to monitor cell phone usage — the results can be used to highlight the extent of the use and reduce it.
- Hardware or network providers can implement call limits, preventing use after a certain period of prolonged use (some video games companies do this in China).

Non-technical solutions

- 'Camps' where cell-phone addicted users are prevented from using their phones may be effective.
- Education about appropriate use (e.g. time limits, times and places that are appropriate for use) may be more effective for most (mildly) addicted users.

This exercise should be marked according to the generic ITGS extended response rubric for SL and HL Paper 1. This can be found in the ITGS Specimen Papers.

Exercise 12-11
Possible answers include:
Advantages

- SMS (text messages) can be sent very cheaply — this helps health officials reach as many people as possible (for example, during awareness campaigns).
- Young people are often very familiar with mobile phone technology — this can help health officials reach this demographic (who may be reluctant to visit a doctor).
- SMS (text messages) can be sent in a variety of languages — this may improve the equality of access in countries where a large variety of languages are spoken (for example, South Africa) but traditional healthcare advice may only be available in one or two languages.
- Mobile phone technology is often very widespread, even in developing countries — this can make it a more effective medium for reaching remote areas who may not have television or Internet access.
- Mobile phones are somewhat "anonymous" - this may encourage people to seek help and advice on conditions they would be embarrassed or unwilling to discuss face to face (for example, HIV testing).
- Modern smart phones can be connected to a variety of sensors that can allow patients to take certain readings (blood pressure, pulse rate) at home and upload to a doctor — this increases the patient's independence and saves time and money on travel.

Disadvantages

- Voice and (especially) text communication are somewhat limited—this may make providing some types of direct individual advice difficult, because the doctor cannot physically examine the patient.
- There may be concerns that patients access inappropriate sources for health advice (such as user-generated advice sites) —this could cause them to self-diagnose and delay proper treatment.

This exercise should be marked according to the generic ITGS extended response rubric for SL and HL Paper 1. This can be found in the ITGS Specimen Papers.

Exercise 12-12

(i) A primary key is a field in a database table [1 mark] which contains a unique value for every record, enabling it to be uniquely identified.[1 mark]

(ii)
When using an opt-in system, no patient data is included in the EMR system [1 mark] unless they give their express consent (typically in writing) for it to be included [1 mark].

Using an opt-out system, all patients' data is included by default [1 mark], unless the patient expressly requests that it is not [1 mark].

b)

- The doctor authenticates himself to the EMR using a password, biometrics, or security token.
- The doctor enters details of the patient he wishes to find (for example, name or social security number).
- These criteria are sent to the server holding the EMR data, which performs a search (query) of all records.
- The record(s) matching the doctor's query are sent back to his computer. If more than one record exists, he selects the right one.
- The patient's information is displayed on screen, with fields including name, gender, date of birth, medical history. This helps verify that the correct record has been selected.
- The doctor is able to view and (depending on his access privileges) edit the data.
- Any changed data is sent to the EMR server and updated on the records there.

c)
Possible answers include:
Security issues

- Data must be held securely on the system / server itself—encrypted to prevent unauthorised access.
- Systems must be protected with authentication systems (such as usernames and passwords or biometrics) to prevent unauthorised access.
- Data in transit from the EMR server to the doctor's client computers / PDAs must be encrypted—for example, using SSL or TLS.
- If data is transmitted over a wireless network, that network must be secured against unauthorised access and must be encrypted using WPA2 to keep data secure.
- Client computers / viewing devices must be configured not to store copies of medical records, which could then be accessed if the device was stolen.
- Servers housing the EMR system must be physically secured—for example, in locked cabinets in locked rooms, with biometric or similar access.
- Any backups of the servers must be encrypted and stored securely (physical security).

Privacy

- There should be different levels of access for different staff members—for example, receptionists should have access to only basic contact details; doctors to more complete records.
- Data should not be shared with third parties (for example, drugs companies) without the patient's express permission.
- The hospital should have a privacy policy in place and train staff to adhere to it.

Integrity

- Appropriate validation checks should be set up on fields to disallow invalid data.
- When accessing or updating records, staff could verify a patient's identity using multiple fields—for example, the name, date of birth, and photo. This prevents alterations to the wrong patient's records.
- Doctors should confirm the patient's details with them during a consultation, rather than relying on the records being accurate.
- Patients should have the right to correct or remove any data that is incorrect.

This exercise should be marked according to the generic ITGS extended response rubric for SL and HL Paper 1. This can be found in the ITGS Specimen Papers.

Exercise 12-13

a)

i) Data logging is the process of using sensors to measure and record data [1 mark] automatically over a period of time [1 mark].

ii)

- Motion sensor – used to determine if the patient is moving or has moved recently.
- Sound sensor – measures sound / noise levels. If a house is very quiet or silent for extended periods of time it may indicate a problem with the patient.
- Temperature sensor – measures the room's temperature to detect any unusual fluctuations (such as a sudden drop) which could cause or indicate a problem with the patient.
- Contact sensors – these can be used on doors in the house or on the refrigerator to determine if they have been opened, which indicates normal activity.

Grade according to the 6 mark Explanation rubric on page 141.

c)

Possible answers include:

Benefits

- Being able to locate a patient immediately reduces the health and safety risks to the patient.
- The tracking systems could be combined with an alert system to notify family members if a patient leaves a certain area—this could further help reduce safety risks to the patient.
- Families members and carers may have increased peace of mind, knowing that they will be able to locate the patient.
- The patient gains some degree of independence—they do not need to be constantly accompanied by carers (depending on the extent of their illness).

Concerns

- It is likely that patient tracking data will be captured continuously, keeping a record of the patients' movement. This is a privacy concern.
- Additional monitoring devices such as cameras create surveillance issues.
- There may be concerns over whether the patient is aware that the cameras are active and medical staff are viewing them at any given time.
- There may be concerns about the installation of cameras in some areas of the house, such as the bathroom or the bedroom.
- There may be concerns that the tracking company sells personal data about the patient and their fami-

lies—for example, to advertisers of related medical products and services.

This exercise should be marked according to the generic ITGS extended response rubric for SL and HL Paper 1. This can be found in the ITGS Specimen Papers.

Exercise 12-14

a)

(i)

Telemedicine is the use of information technology to provide medical care [1 mark] when the patient and doctor are in separate geographical locations.[1 mark]

(ii)

- A video camera
- Microphone so the patient can hear the doctor and vice versa.
- Video camera to allow the doctor to see the patient and their symptoms (possibly vice versa too).
- A high bandwidth (broadband) connection to allow the sending of real time video data.

Award 1 mark for the item identified and 1 mark for a description, up to 4 marks.

b)

Possible answers include:

- Patients' privacy must be respected. Hospital staff must not reveal sensitive data online, including the patient's name and medical history.
- The online forum is not a substitute for consultation with a real doctor. The hospital would need to make this policy clear to patients to avoid problems with patients who fall ill after failing to see a doctor.
- Staff should not provide direct, individual advice or diagnosis, but instead should provide general health care education (for example, advice about coping with certain disabilities, or general healthy lifestyle advice).
- The moderators / forum staff should contact emergency services if they suspect a life-threatening emergency—for example, an accident or a person who appears suicidal.

Award 1 mark for the clause identified and 1 mark for an explanation, up to 6 marks.

c)

Possible answers include:

Benefits

- Providing educational advice online may reduce visits to hospitals for relatively minor issues that do not need the attention of a doctor.
- In emergencies (for example, flu epidemics), citizens can be advised to remain at home and follow online advice—limiting their exposure and the spread of the disease.
- People may be more willing to seek advice online that talk to a doctor in person, especially if the advice relates to an embarrassing problem.
- Online communities can provide psychological and practical support for people with similar conditions (for example, coping with a sick relative) - this help can be hard to find elsewhere.

Drawbacks

- The reliability of the advice is likely to be a concern unless the site is operated by a recognised and trusted medical organisation.
- It is possible that patients will misunderstand advice and guidance given online.
- There is a danger that patients will use online advice to self-diagnose—either convincing themselves they have a much more serious illness than in reality, or convincing themselves that they are not sick (and thus delaying treatment).

This exercise should be marked according to the generic ITGS extended response rubric for SL and HL Paper 1. This can be found in the ITGS Specimen Papers.

Chapter 13
Home & Leisure

Chapter 13 Solutions

Exercise 13-1

Grade according to the rubric on page 137.

Exercise 13-2
Possible answers include:

- Games companies can be required by law to limit the number of hours of continuous playing by one account.
- *PC-bangs* (cyber cafes) where games are played can be required to limit their customers to a certain number of hours of use (this could be enforced by monitoring software).
- *PC-bangs* (cyber cafes) where games are played can be required to verify the age of their customers—for example, keeping the most vulnerable groups such as children away from the systems during certain hours (such as during the school day).
- Parents can install filters on their children's computers to prevent access to particularly problematic sites or games (or limit access to certain times).
- 'Camps' where Internet addicted users are prevented from using their phones may be effective.
- Education about appropriate use (e.g. time limits), may be effective for mildly addicted users.

This exercise should be marked according to the generic ITGS extended response rubric for SL and HL Paper 1. This can be found in the ITGS Specimen Papers.

Exercise 13-3
Possible answers include:

- Governments can take responsibility for educating their citizens—especially young people—about the negative health effects of excessive games playing.
- PC-café owners can take responsibility by implementing measures (such as time limits) to reduce the incidence of unhealthy playing habits in their premises.
- Games companies can take responsibility by implementing measures like time limits on their accounts.
- Parents can take responsibility by being aware of their children's Internet use (perhaps through logging software) and providing firm rules and guidance.
- Parents can take responsibility by implementing technical solutions such as the blocking of troublesome sites.

- Users themselves can take responsibility by attempting to deal with their problem by reducing time spent online, or engaging in other offline activities.

This exercise should be marked according to the generic ITGS extended response rubric for SL and HL Paper 1. This can be found in the ITGS Specimen Papers.

Exercise 13-4

- Adult users could be banned from using the site. This could be made clear on the sign-up page.
- Adult users could be allowed on the site but made to verify their identity– for example, only teachers signing up from a .edu email address could be allowed.
- Conversations or interactions between adult users and children could be prevented. This would stop potential predators from contacting children.
- Before a child user makes a friendship or connection with another user, the connection could be manually approved by a trusted adult (such as a parent or a virtual world member of staff).
- Analytical software can automatically monitor conversations and behaviour for potential problems – such as users who only attempt to befriend young girls.
- For children, logs of all their activity could be made available to their parents. They could use these to look for signs of anything inappropriate.
- The profiles of children can be made private automatically – preventing other users from seeing personal information such as their name or photo, which could be later misused.
- The virtual world could ban certain types of user-generated content, such as images. This prevents users uploading certain unsuitable content (for example, pornography) for other users to see.
- Facilities to report inappropriate activity should be easily accessible (for example, prominent and on every screen). This makes it easier for users to report anything inappropriate and get it stopped.
- Monitoring software can automatically check interactions and conversations for particular words or phrases – interactions can then be blocked or sent to a human for review.

Award 1 mark for the technique identified and 1 mark for a description, up to 6 marks.

Exercise 13-5
Possible answers include:

Human editors

- Can select a range of stories, including less usual or more surprising articles.
- Can—and do—have biases stemming from political or financial influence, or simply personal interest.

Social news

- 'Popular' news appears first—but this may not present all sides of a story. Other, less popular viewpoints are likely to be lost.
- Popular stories are likely to reflect the interests of the site's users, which in turn attracts more like-minded users and thus continues to present the news that people 'want' to see.
- Some social news systems can be 'gamed' - people with hidden agendas can influence the ranking of a news item.

Automated editors

- 'Popular' news appears first—but this may not present all sides of a story. Other, less popular viewpoints are likely to be lost.
- The metrics used for assessing an article's 'importance' may be closed and unavailable for public scrutiny.
- The metrics used for assessing an article's importance may take into account questionable sources—for example, the number of links to the article created on social networks.
- Automated editors may use the viewer's previous reading habits to suggest personalised news stories—but this may result in hiding contrasting views and opinions.

Exercise 13-6
Students should discuss a range of changes that may be made to the images and how this affects their accuracy.

Students should consider:

- Enhancements may enable the viewer to discern data that was previously invisible to the human eye.
- Image detail cannot be created from nothing: if it is not present in the original film, it is lost.
- Digital enhancement techniques such as sharpening take average values of surrounding pixels and create 'new' data that did not previously exist in the image.
- Some enhancements may be more extreme that others: for example, colourising the footage might be considered an extreme alteration.

- It is important to notify the viewer that the image has been manipulated, and how.

Exercise 13-7
Possible answers include:

- Search engines such as Google crawl and index the web automatically; file sharing sites often have facilities for users to upload links to pirated content (such as Torrent files).
- Search engines aim to index material on a wide range of topics (effectively, all public web pages); file sharing sites typically encourage the sharing of links to illegal copies of files.
- Search engines will typically also index file sharing sites, providing links to them for relevant search results.
- Search engines typically provide a feature to request the removal of content from their results pages; file sharing sites sometimes do this too.

This exercise should be marked according to the generic ITGS extended response rubric for SL and HL Paper 1. This can be found in the ITGS Specimen Papers.

Exercise 13-8
Technologies students might consider for item identification include:

- OCR (Optical Character Recognition) – for reading some basic text from an image (such as a shop sign).
- Mapping data – existing digital maps contain a great deal of information about the world. These can be combined with GPS and compasses to determine the user's surroundings.
- GPS (Global Positioning System) – to determine location and narrow down possibilities based on mapping data.
- Compass – to determine the direction the user is facing and narrow down possibilities based on mapping data.
- Ultrasonic sensors could be used to detect objects – for example, in the room mapping scenario for fire fighters.

Grade according to the 6 mark Explanation rubric on page 141.

Exercise 13-9
- Care must be taken not to damage the artwork during the moving or scanning process (for example, dropping, or fading due to bright light).

- The resolution of the digital copy. This should as high as possible to ensure that the digital copy is an accurate reproduction of the original.
- Intellectual property rights. The intellectual property rights for the artwork may be held by a third party, and these could be violated if unauthorised digital copies of the work are made.

Grade according to the 6 mark Explanation rubric on page 141.

Exercise 13-10
Possible answers include:
Benefits
- Identity and age verification could help reduce problems related to online grooming / online predators—virtual worlds could automatically limit (or monitor) contact between children and adults.
- Incidents of disruptive behaviour—abuse, bullying, 'trolling', and spam may be reduced if users are required to reveal their identity.

Risks
- People may not wish to reveal their identity online, or may want to use different identities in different virtual worlds or communities.
- There may be especial concern about revealing the online identity of children using the system.
- Using the same (real) identity on multiple systems creates a trail of activity, which could lead to identity theft.
- Accurate identification verification is very hard to perform—requiring government-issued documents such as passports would involve uploading a great deal of sensitive personal data to the virtual world provider—this creates further privacy risks.
- Certain users (for example, anti-government campaigners, democracy campaigners, civil rights campaigners) may have their safety put at risk if they are required to reveal their identity online.
- Limiting adult-child contacts may cause problems in some areas—such as teachers using virtual worlds with students.
- Limiting adult-child contacts automatically gives children the false impression that all adults are harmful.

This exercise should be marked according to the generic ITGS extended response rubric for SL and HL Paper 1. This can be found in the ITGS Specimen Papers.

Exercise 13-11
a)
i)
Possible answers include:
- Via the organisation's web site
- Via a social network feed (Twitter, Facebook)
- Via an RSS feed
- Via a news aggregation site

ii)
- The amount of storage space available / the bandwidth of the network being used – some file formats use compression which reduce these requirements.
- The type of compression used (lossless or lossy) – as each is suited to different types of image.
- The amount of lossy compression used (if any) – since excessive compression can significantly reduce image detail.

Do not allow: the resolution of the image, since the file format does not affect this.

Award 1 mark for the method identified and 1 mark for a description, up to 4 marks.

b)
- Manipulated images should be avoided – the newspaper should avoid images it believes or should reasonably believe have been digitally manipulated. Using such images could significantly harm the reputation of the newspaper.
- Images should still follow the newspaper's policies on unacceptable content – for example, excessive gore or images which invade privacy. Otherwise the newspaper could be held legally responsible, even if it did not take the photograph itself.
- They should only use images they have permission to distribute – for example, public domain images, Creative Commons images, or copyrighted images where the copyright holder has given permission for reproduction. Failure to follow these rules could result in legal action against the newspaper for violation of intellectual property rights.
- Attribution and acknowledgement – the newspaper should acknowledge the source of the photograph and provide a link to the source (if online). This is good practice which improves the reputation of the newspaper by acknowledging the contributions its readers make.

Grade according to the 6 mark Explanation rubric on page 141.

c)

Possible answers include:

Benefits

- In some situation citizens are the only people present to document an event (for example, in the London Underground tube bombings).

- Even if regular journalists are present, citizen journalists may provide another viewpoint on a subject (for example, documenting the experience of the spectators during the Olympic games).

- Material provided by citizen journalists may be available very cheaply.

Concerns

- The quality of the images from a citizen journalist may be lower—for example, such images are often recorded with mobile phones or compact cameras.

- Citizen journalists lack professional standards and guidance—for example, they may invade the privacy of injured victims by taking and publishing photographs of them at their most vulnerable.

- There can be a conflict between a desire to document an event and helping people who may be injured.

- The increased use of citizen journalists (who are paid less than professional journalists) could reduce the demand for professional journalists.

This exercise should be marked according to the generic ITGS extended response rubric for SL and HL Paper 1. This can be found in the ITGS Specimen Papers.

Exercise 13-12

a)

i)

Intellectual property refers to non-physical items [1 mark] – creations of the mind such as images, stories, films, and music [1 mark].

ii)

Possible answers include:

- High bandwidth Internet connections have enabled large files to be transferred relatively quickly.

- Modern compression technologies allow entire films to be compressed to a relatively small file size – around 700MB for 90 minutes of video.

- Peer-to-peer networks allow users to transfer files directly to each other, making it harder for authorities to shut them down.

Award 1 mark for the method identified and 1 mark for a description, up to 4 marks.

b)

Possible answers include:

- The video quality needs to be considered (particularly for streaming content). Lower bandwidth Internet connections may be unable to cope with streaming high quality content. However, reducing the video quality may give a negative impression of their content.

- Copy protection measures such as Digital Rights Management (DRM) might be considered. These technologies can help reduce the financial losses caused by online piracy. However, many genuine users do not like the restrictions these systems place on them.

- The price of the content must be considered. There needs to be a balance between the price users pay for a digital copy of the product (perhaps only a single view) and the price they pay for a physical DVD/Blu-ray disk. If the price is too high, users are more likely to opt for the physical product.

- Licensing issues need to be considered—for example, the distributor may only have the rights to distribute the content in some countries, and must therefore prevent downloads by users from other countries.

Grade according to the 6 mark Explanation rubric on page 141.

c)

Possible answers include:

- Governments can pass laws requiring Internet Service Providers to filter access to sites containing illegal material.

- Governments can work with media industry bodies to educate users about copyright infringement and its negative impacts.

- Governments can work with media industry bodies to perform software licence audits on large organisations—to encourage them to use legally acquired software.

- Governments can work with law enforcement to shut down web hosts that host sites containing illegal material—though often this can be difficult if such sites are located overseas.

This exercise should be marked according to the generic ITGS extended response rubric for SL and HL Paper 1. This can be found in the ITGS Specimen Papers.

Chapter 14
Politics & Government

Chapter 14 Solutions

Exercise 14-1

In this exercise students should consider the wide range of content that may be deemed "unsuitable" by various cultures or communities. This is a good opportunity to discuss the Globalisation and Cultural Diversity social / ethical issue.

Examples might include information about: racism, violence, sex education, abortion, gay rights, religion, drug use, revisionist history (for example, Holocaust denial), pro-suicide sites, violations of privacy, incitements to violence, pro-democracy sites, anti-government sites, terrorist sites.

Exercise 14-2

While discussing this question students should consider examples of the following issues:

- How filtering can prevent access to information that may help our understanding of the world (for example, alternative viewpoints of events).
- How we can know if our Internet access is filtered (for example, whether we see a "blocked" message when accessing a banned site, or a normal error message).

Exercise 14-3

Students should consider technologies including:

- Social networks
- Blogs
- Micro-blogs
- RSS feeds
- Email mailing lists
- Photo sharing sites
- Video sharing sites
- Web sites

Grade according to the rubric on page 138.

Exercise 14-4

Possible answers include:

- Water installations
- Electricity grids
- Power plants
- Telephone networks (especially emergency calls)
- Hospital networks
- Military bases
- Scientific research
- Military contractors
- Banks and financial institutions
- Government web sites
- Media organisations

Exercise 14-5

Possible answers include:

- Counter-espionage (using cyber-warfare tactics against possible threats).
- Strong authentication methods on secure systems (such as biometrics or two-factor authentication).
- Encryption of data on key systems.
- Protection of networks using firewalls.
- Physically isolating secure systems from the Internet.
- Policies enforcing strong security procedures.

Grade according to the 6 mark Explanation rubric on page 141.

Exercise 14-6

Possible answers include:

- Accessing systems from many (geographically separated) devices increases the number of possible attack vectors (such as network compromise).
- It is hard to monitor the use of remote computers and networks to ensure users are following security and privacy policies.
- The sheer number of users increased the number of potential victims (for example, of phishing attacks).
- A single compromised device used to access the database could breach security of the entire database.
- It is harder to ensure so many people follow security and privacy policies.
- It might be harder to identify individuals who are breaching security or policy procedures.
- There may be a higher risk of a 'rogue' employee who deliberately leak data in order to damage the employer.
- Large amounts of data, even if anonymous, can be combined with other records to identify individuals.

This exercise should be marked according to the generic ITGS extended response rubric for SL and HL Paper 1. This can be found in the ITGS Specimen Papers.

Exercise 14-7

Possible answers include:

- There may be consequences or significance to the data that is unknown to those releasing it (for example, revealing the identity of informers or undercover agents) - this could put others in harm's way.

- Leaked information may be misused by third parties (for example, terrorists) - this could seriously harm others.
- The released data may be incomplete or taken out of context—people mentioned in leaked documents may be incorrectly considered guilty by association.
- Certain types of information may infringe on the privacy rights of those mentioned in the leaked material—for example, releasing financial records or communication transcripts.
- It may be argued that releasing the material is in the public interest (for example, if it exposes government corruption).
- It could be argued that governments are servants of the people; that people have a right to know how their elected officials behave.
- Leaking of information about certain events (for example, torture of prisoners) could bring it into the media spotlight and potentially stop it.
- Such leaks may be the only scrutiny that certain organisations or individuals receive.

This exercise should be marked according to the generic ITGS extended response rubric for SL and HL Paper 1. This can be found in the ITGS Specimen Papers.

Exercise 14-8
Possible answers include:

- Encrypted communication channels mean that the source of the data cannot be identified. This makes it harder for the authorities to track the source and prevent it leaking further information.
- Overseas hosting facilities mean the authorities have no legal jurisdiction – and law enforcement in the host country is often less strict.
- Mirror sites contain copies of the original site – this means that even if one site is shut down by the authorities, other copies continue to be freely accessible on the Internet.
- Peer-to-peer file sharing sites mean files are not centrally hosted—this makes it much harder for authorities to shut down.

Grade according to the 4 mark Explanation rubric on page 140.

Exercise 14-9
Possible answers include:

Arguments in favour of ISPs being held responsible

- ISPs are in a perfect position to monitor communication and filter out illegal content.
- Filtering content via ISPs may be more effective than attempting to take-down content hosts (who may be based overseas, outside legal jurisdiction).
- A law would ensure that all ISPs block the same content—a concerted effort could seriously reduce the distribution of illegal content.

Arguments against ISPs being held responsible

- ISPs would be required to monitor all users' network activity to look for illegal activity—many would consider this a significant breach of privacy.
- The cost of monitoring every data packet sent over the ISP's network would be extremely high.
- Monitoring every packet of data sent could adversely affect network speed.
- An ISP's reputation may be harmed if its users become aware that their activities are being monitored.
- ISPs are not law enforcement agencies.
- Such attempts at monitoring could easily be circumvented by users who employ encryption.

This exercise should be marked according to the generic ITGS extended response rubric for SL and HL Paper 1. This can be found in the ITGS Specimen Papers.

Exercise 14-10
Possible answers include:

- Public facilities such as libraries or schools could provide free Internet access – this enables users without access at home to view government sites.
- Printed copies of material can be made available. These could be accessible at public libraries or local government offices.
- Telephone services could be set up—citizens could call in and request a copy of the data they require is sent to them via the postal service.

Award 1 mark for the method identified and 1 mark for a description, up to 4 marks.

Exercise 14-11

Technology: Wikis

Possible uses:

- Housing drafts of proposed legislation—these could be edited or added to by various citizens, ensuring involvement in the law-making process.
- Citizen-edited sites that propose areas the government should address or suggest policy changes.

Technology: Blogs

Possible uses:

- Posting the latest news or policies information—blogs can be set up to deal with specific individual issues such as the environment, employment, or healthcare.

Technology: RSS feeds

Possible uses:

- These can be used in conjunction with blogs, wikis, or other web 2.0 technologies—they allow citizens to subscribe to the content, thus receiving updates as soon as they are released.

Technology: Streaming video

Possible uses:

- Live broadcasting of speeches, parliamentary debates, and news bulletins—users can watch these on mobile devices if they are not near a TV.

Technology: Podcasts

Possible uses:

- Audio and video podcasts can be used to archive key events—political debates, speeches, and interviews. These can be viewed on demand by citizens.

Technology: Mashups

Possible uses:

- Government crime data can be overlaid onto mapping data to reveal crime hotspots.
- Government spending data can be overlaid onto mapping data to show the extent of investment in each area.
- Health data (for example, obesity levels) can be overlaid onto mapping data to reveal health hotspots (and areas with health problems).

Grade according to the 4 mark Explanation rubric on page 140. (Applied to each technology)

Exercise 14-12

Possible answers include:

Arguments in favour

- Biometrics can be used at the canteen and the library—this may be more convenient than carrying money or identification cards around.
- Parents may be able to control their child's spending habits—for example, controlling the amount of money they can spend each day at the canteen.
- Parents may be able to monitor their child's spending habits—for example, checking the types of snacks they bought if the system allows online record access.
- Attendance records may be more accurate—precise times are recorded and there is less chance of students being misidentified.
- There is less chance of theft or bullying since students will not need to carry money to school.
- There is less chance of loss since children will not need to carry money to school.

Arguments against

- Biometric data is inherently sensitive data—if lost (through a security breach), it is irrevocable.
- Schools may not have the knowledge or infrastructure to store biometric data securely.
- There may be concerns over privacy if records of attendance, location, and purchases are kept on the system—it needs to be clear how this data could be used.
- The setup cost of the system and the readers may be high—this may be passed on to parents (school fees) or affect students (reduced money for resources).

Do not accept answers that address benefits or concerns for the school—answers should focus on the students and the parents.

Grade according to the 6 mark Explanation rubric on page 141.

Exercise 14-13

a)

(i) Cyber-warfare is the use of computer hacking techniques by a nation [1 mark] to attack the computers and infrastructure of an enemy [1 mark].

(ii)

Possible answers include:

- Keyword filter – this scans all content for the presence of certain keywords (defined by the system administrator) and blocks pages containing them.
- Black list – a list of web sites to which access is

blocked. Access is allowed to sites not on the list.

- White list – a list of web sites to which users are allowed access. Other websites not on the list are typically blocked.

Award 1 mark for the method identified and 1 mark for a description, up to 4 marks.

b)
For a keyword filter:
- The filter is configured (the banned keywords are entered) on the Internet gateway (server).
- A user on a computer tries to access a certain web site.
- The Internet gateway retrieves the web page and scans it for the presence of the banned words.
- If the banned words are found on the page, access is denied and the user is sent a "page blocked" page.
- If the banned words are not found, the web page sent to the user.

For a black list:
- The filter is configured (the list of banned sites is entered) on the Internet gateway (server).
- A user on a computer tries to access a web site.
- The Internet gateway checks the URL or IP address of the web site against the black list.
- If the site is found on the list, access is denied and the user is sent a "page blocked" page.
- If the site is not on the list, the web page is retrieved as normal and sent to the user.

For a white list:
- The filter is configured (the list of allowed sites is entered) on the Internet gateway (server).
- A user on a computer tries to access a web site.
- The Internet gateway checks the URL or IP address of the web site against the white list.
- If the site is found on the list, access is granted and the page is retrieved.
- If the site is not on the list, access is denied and the user is sent a "page blocked" page.

Grade according to the 6 mark Explanation rubric on page 141.

c)
Possible answers include:
Arguments in favour of individual filtering
- Individual families and businesses will have different filtering requirements—some may want more content filtered and others may want less filtered.
- Filtering can be turned on and off as required (for

example, for adults who want to use the Internet).
- It may be easier to block and unblock sites (for example, false positives or false negatives).

Arguments against of individual filtering
- Few people will have the time, skill, or knowledge to configure filtering on their systems, thus reducing its effectiveness.
- Individuals may be given a false sense of security—believing their children or networks are unable to access any undesirable material (in reality, false negatives will always occur).

Arguments in favour of governmental filtering
- No technical expertise or knowledge is required on behalf of individual users.
- Lists of blocked sites remain consistent across all devices—this means children cannot access blocked content at their friends' houses, for example.
- Some content is extremely harmful and blocking it may be required by law (for example, hate material or terrorist material).

Arguments against governmental filtering
- There is a risk that filtering will not be performed transparently—that the government may start to expand the list of 'undesirable' content to include other categories (such as political opponents).
- It may be difficult or time-consuming to unblock incorrectly blocked sites.
- Parents may believe they are absolved of their parental responsibilities because the government is filtering harmful content for them.
- Nation-wide filtering may conflict with free-speech rights.
- Deciding what is 'appropriate' and what is 'inappropriate' is a difficult decision that has different answers for different people—the government's decision will not suit everyone (or possibly, anyone).

This exercise should be marked according to the generic ITGS extended response rubric for SL and HL Paper 1. This can be found in the ITGS Specimen Papers.

Exercise 14-14
a)
(i)
An avatar is a small image [1 mark] that users on virtual worlds and social networks use to represent themselves [1 mark].

(ii)

Virtual reality immerses players in an environment that is entirely digital (virtual) [1 mark], with the player being able to move and interact with virtual objects in the world [1 mark]. Mixed reality uses a combination of virtual environment and the physical world [1 mark] to create a more realistic environment where the player interacts with real and virtual objects [1 mark].

b)

Possible answers include:

- The simulator can be configured for any conditions (for example, night time, low visibility) without the need to wait for them to happen in real life.
- Many simulators use real life input and output devices (or objects in the case of mixed reality), improving the realism of the training.
- There is less risk of injury or death—for example, in military exercises there is no risk of injury from stray ammunition.
- Software simulations allow for more realistic situations (such as moving targets and civilians) than traditional wooden targets.
- Exercises can be recorded (including 'invisible' data about the users) and analysed in detail later.
- Exercises can be repeated exactly many times.
- The costs of using a simulation may be lower than the cost of building, maintaining, and operating physical training environments.

Grade according to the 6 mark Explanation rubric on page 141.

c)

Possible answers include:

- The system must fall-back to a safe mode if communication between the UAV and the pilot is broken.
- The communication lag between the UAV and the pilot must be minimal (both for sending video feedback and receiving the pilot's commands).
- The communication network between the pilot and UAV must be secure to prevent unauthorised access to the communication channels (which could result in commands being interrupted or inserted).
- The image / video quality from the UAV must be sufficient to allow the pilot to clearly see the ground—this is necessary for correct identification of targets.
- The software in the UAV needs to be extremely reliable / redundant systems need to be used that can take over in the event of a primary system failure.
- The system needs to be designed in such a way that only the pilot is able to fire the weapon systems.

This exercise should be marked according to the generic ITGS extended response rubric for SL and HL Paper 1. This can be found in the ITGS Specimen Papers.

Exercise 14-15

a)

i)

RSS (Really Simple Syndication) is a push technology [1 mark] used to retrieve the latest updates from a web site without needing to visit the site itself. [1 mark]

ii)

Electronic voting refers to the use of any computerised machine to process votes [1 mark] – whether it is casting and counting the votes, or just counting them [1 mark]. Online voting is the process of casting votes [1 mark] over a network (typically the Internet) [1 mark].

b)

Possible answers include:

- A physical token (for example a smart card) can be connect to a computer—this authenticates the card as belonging to somebody who has the right to vote.
- The card could use public key encryption systems to digitally sign the vote that is cast—this further authenticates the user and authenticates the card as a genuine card.
- The smart card should have some form of authentication mechanism (such as a PIN or a biometric reader) - this authenticates the person connecting it to the computer as the owner of the card.
- Voting should take place using software that is digitally signed—this authenticates the software as genuine and not imposter software that may alter votes.
- The voting server and voting software need to exchange digital signatures—this ensures they are communicating with genuine systems and not imposters.
- The connection between the voting software and the voting server must be encrypted—this prevents alteration of the data during transit.

Grade according to the 6 mark Explanation rubric on page 141.

c)

Possible answers include:

Reliability and integrity

- The vote tabulation software needs to be tested to ensure it counts votes correctly and reliably.
- Vote tabulation software needs to be verifiable—it should be possible to confirm that it has not changed since it was created (by unauthorised users).

- The internal operation of the vote tabulation software should be transparent—perhaps by making the source code open.
- Input devices (such as touch screens) need to be correctly configured to ensure they register inputs in the correct places.

Security
- The vote tabulation software needs to be secure from unauthorised access and tampering.
- The voting machines need to be physically secured to prevent unauthorised access to the hardware and software.
- The network communication between online voting software and the voting server needs to be encrypted to prevent unauthorised access.

Equality of Access
- Electronic and online voting systems can be made accessible for disabled users—for example, through a variety of accessibility software and hardware.
- Officials must be careful to ensure users without a computer or Internet access are not disenfranchised.

This exercise should be marked according to the generic ITGS extended response rubric for SL and HL Paper 1. This can be found in the ITGS Specimen Papers.

Chapter 15
IT Systems in Organisations

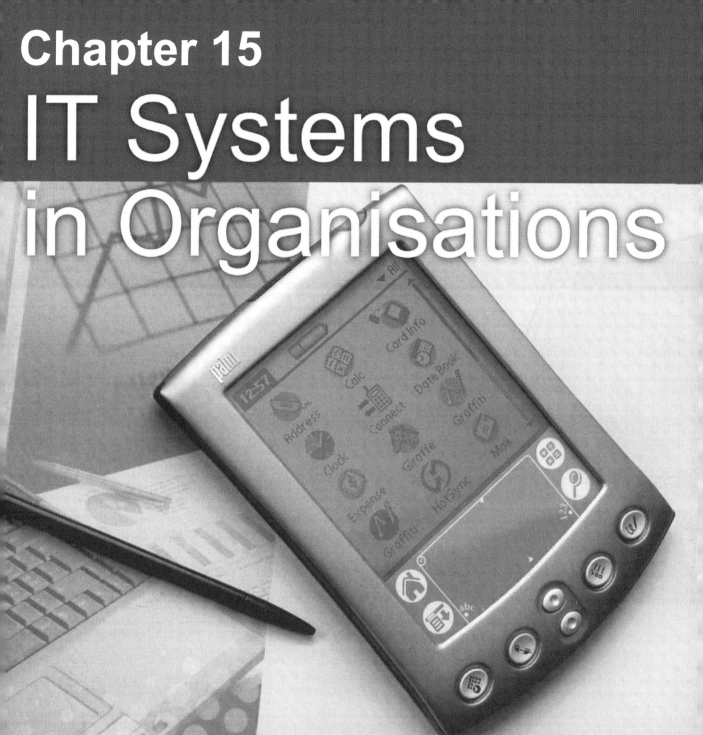

Chapter 15 Solutions

Exercise 15-1
Scenario 1 (Bicycle rental)

Sample system context diagram:

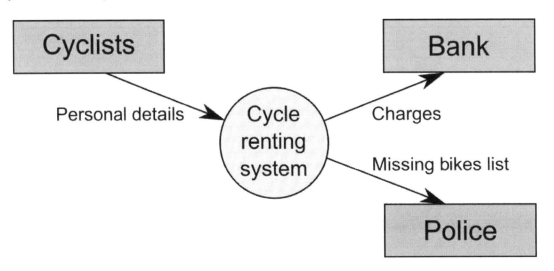

Sample Data Flow Diagram (DFD):

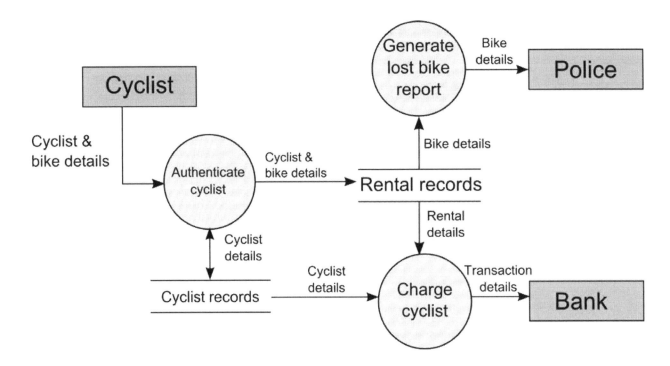

Sample Entity Relationship Diagram (ERD):

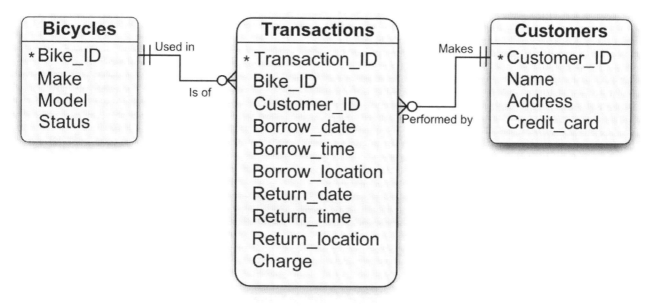

Notes:

- *Tables may have slightly different names (e.g. 'Transactions' could be called 'Rentals' or similar).*
- *Bicycles.Make and Bicycles.Model are illustrative and not essential to the diagram.*

Exercise 15-1
Scenario 2 (E-commerce web site)

Sample system context diagram:

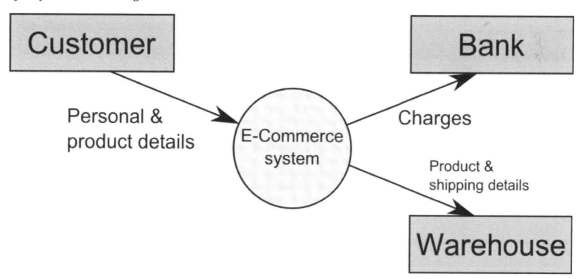

Sample Data Flow Diagram (DFD):

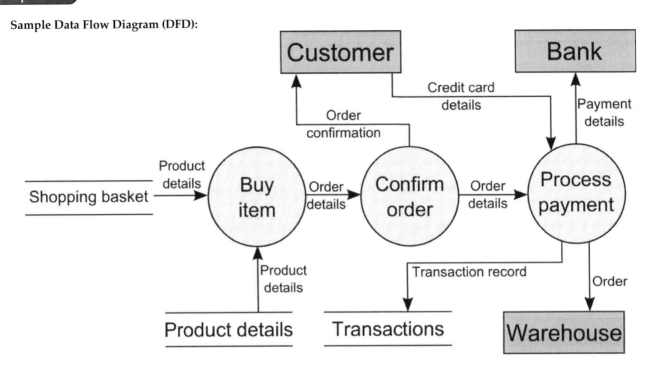

Sample Entity Relationship Diagram (ERD):

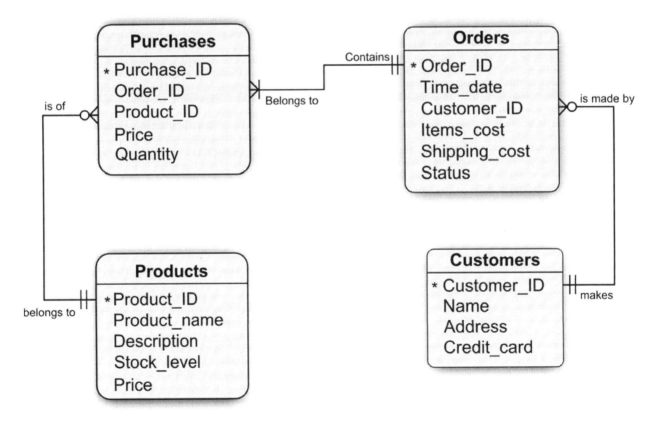

Notes:

- *The Purchases table contains the price field (seemingly duplicated) because we want to know the price the user paid at the time, which may be different from the current price.*
- *Naming of the Purchases table is slightly awkward. Here, one order consists of several purchases. Each purchase is of one product (though the quantity may be more than one).*
- *The Purchase_ID primary key exists to simplify the relationship with the Orders table (removing the need for a composite key of consisting of Order_ID and Product_ID).*

Exercise 15-2

There are several resources relating to the FBI Sentinel project available on the ITGS textbook web site (www.itgstextbook.com). Issues encountered include:

- The project was over budget
- The project did not meet deadlines
- Private sector consultants were brought in partway through development to get the project back on track
- The project was switched from a waterfall-based methodology to an Agile methodology partway through development (and is credited with ensuring the project was actually finished).
- A load-test of the system in October 2011 failed (mainly due to running the system on old hardware).

Several of these mistakes were made previously in the Virtual Case File system. However, Sentinel was somewhat finished and became available to all FBI agents in July 2012.

Exercise 15-3

Possible answers include:

- A direct changeover in this instance was certainly inappropriate. The direct changeover exacerbated existing problems in the system (such as software bugs and the inability to deal with a high call load).
- If a parallel or phased changeover had been used, these problems would have been noted at some point during the deployment, before the old system was completely abandoned.
- Instead, direct changeover meant that when the system failed there was no backup system available, forcing dispatchers to use paper tracking methods and resulting in the unacceptable delays to ambulance dispatches.

Grade according to the 4 mark Explanation rubric on page 140.

Exercise 15-4

a)
See sample Gantt chart diagram on page 104.

Grade as follows:

- *Each task should be shown and correctly positioned (students should use their own discretion for selecting a time frame) [1 mark]*
- *Milestones must be present (and distinguished from tasks) (Handover) [1 mark]*
- *The scale should be correct and the dates clear [1 mark]*
- *Each stage of the PDLC should be complete before the next one commences (e.g. analysis should finish before design starts). [1 mark]*
- *Sensible date ranges should be chosen for each stage (each stage could be roughly equal, or the design and implementation stages could be slightly longer than other stages). [2 marks]*

b)
See sample Gantt chart diagram on page 104.

Grade as follows:

- *Each task should be shown and correctly positioned (students should use their own discretion for selecting a time frame) [1 mark]*
- *Milestones must be present (and distinguished from tasks) (Handover) [1 mark]*
- *The scale should be correct and the dates clear [1 mark]*
- *The project should be divided into modules (e.g. storing details, reporting of grades, entry of grades). [1 mark]*
- *Each stage of the PDLC should occur several times: once for each module that is shown on the scale. [2 marks]*

c)
See sample PERT chart on page 105.

Grade as follows:

- *Each task is shown and correctly named [1 mark]*
- *Each task has the correct start and end dates [1 mark]*
- *Each task has the correct duration [1 mark]*
- *The tasks are in the correct sequence [2 marks]*
- *The critical path is clearly indicated [1 mark]*

Exercise 15-4 Sample Gantt chart (Waterfall approach)

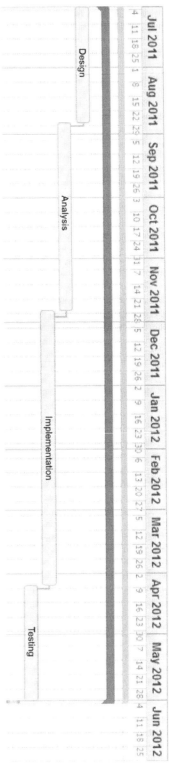

Exercise 15-4 Sample Gantt chart (Agile approach)

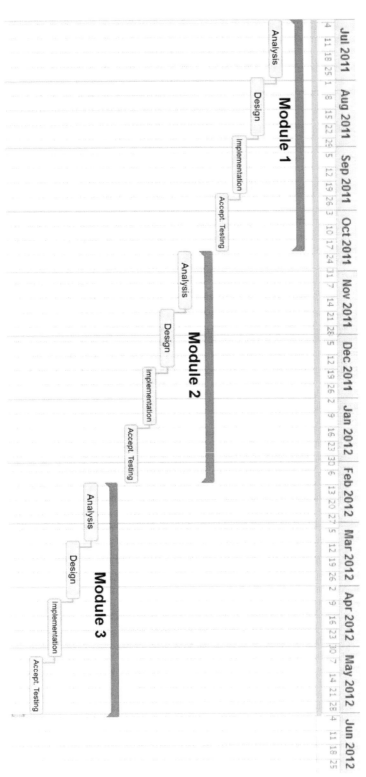

Exercise 15-4 Sample PERT chart (Waterfall approach)

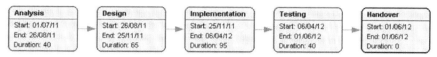

Exercise 15-5

See sample diagrams below.

Grade ERD as follows:

- *The correct attributes have been selected and included in the correct entities. [2 marks]*
- *The relationships between entities are correctly indicated and labelled [2 marks]*
- *The cardinalities of the relationships are correctly indicated [2 mark]*

Grade system context diagram as follows:

- *External entities (sinks) are correctly identified [1 mark]*
- *Incoming and outgoing data flows are correctly identified (including direction) and labelled. [3 marks]*

Notes:

- *It is assumed that each appointment involves only one patient and only one doctor.*
- *The separate Treatments table is required because one appointment could result in multiple treatments.*

Exercise 15-5 Sample ERD

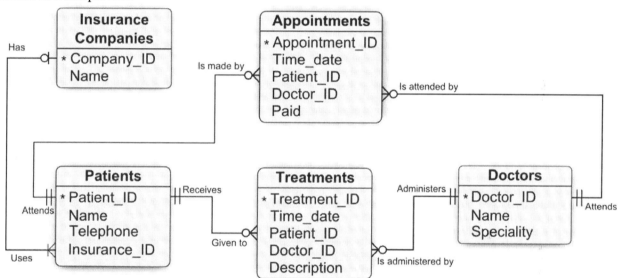

Exercise 15-4 Sample system context diagram

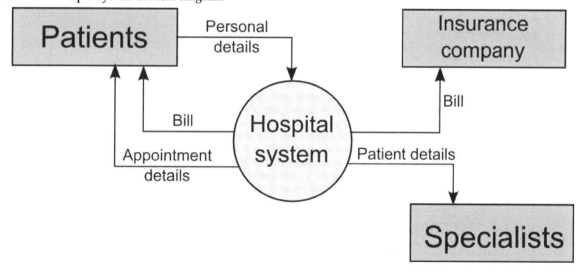

Exercise 15-6
Sample Gantt chart:

| Sep 2011 | Oct 2011 | Nov 2011 | Dec 2011 | Jan 2012 | Feb 2012 | Mar 2012 | Apr 2012 | May 2012 |

Analysis (Jane Pear)

Design (Lucy Riess)

Development (Sam Tallen)

Testing (Jack Patiol)

Acceptance (Clarence West)

Exercise 15-6
See sample Gantt chart above.

Grade as follows:
- *Each task should be shown, correctly positioned, and correctly labelled [1 mark]*
- *The scale should be correct and the dates clear [2 marks]*
- *The name of the individual responsible should be clearly indicated in or near each task. [1 mark]*

Exercise 15-7
a)
i)
A beta test is the testing of a new software system by actual users [1 mark] rather than testers within the development company [1 mark].

ii)
Possible answers include:
- Definition of the project goals—a clear definition of what the project is intended to achieved.
- Definition of project scope—determining the boundaries between responsibility of the project and the responsibilities of other systems outside the project.
- Data collection about the current system—performed to understand the current system, how it works, and how it is used.
- Requirements specification—a formal description of the behaviour / features the project should include.
- Identification of possible solutions—a list of possible ways to achieve the requirements specification.
- Feasibility study—an examination of the possible solutions to decide whether their benefits outweigh their costs. (Cost-benefit analysis).
- Justification of a chosen solution—the selection of a feasible solution and an explanation of how it can achieve the project's goals.
- Creation of a project plan / schedule—a detailed plan of what should be done, when, and by whom.

Award 1 mark for identifying the step and 1 mark for a description, up to 4 marks.

b)
Possible answers include:
- Important aspects of a project (such as cost or time) can be tracked—this means the project's progress can be compared with the plan to assess its performance. (Managed level)
- Standard processes and procedures can be defined for the whole organisation—ensuring a consistent approach that ensures improvements to processes affect everybody. (Defined level)
- Statistical data can be used to assess projects—this can be used to identify and address areas of concern, such as projects that are significantly over time or budget. (Qualitatively Managed)
- An organisation reflects upon its performance—this enables "fine-tuning" of processes and procedures, and allows small incremental improvements to be made. (Optimising)

Award 1 mark for the benefit identified and 1 mark for the explanation, up to 6 marks.

c)
Possible answers include:
Benefits of the agile model
- Evidence of progress is quickly visible—prototypes can be given to clients.
- Problems with the requirements can be identified and addressed earlier in the development cycle.
- Client feedback can be acquired very quickly.
- Client can be more involved in the process.
- Changes in requirements can be more easily accommodated.

Drawbacks of the agile mode
- Lack of an overall design—can make it harder to

accommodate larger changes later (during maintenance).

- Can lead to poor quality code—where functionality may be duplicated.
- Can lead to re-writing of code.
- The client must work very closely with the development team (meeting frequently).
- The resultant project may lack sufficient design documentation.

Benefits of the waterfall model
- A thorough analysis and design should identify problems / confusions early on in the cycle.
- Clear designs are produced and are easily followed.
- Encourages documentation of the project process.

Drawbacks of the waterfall model
- Changes in the requirements are harder to accommodate—and are more expensive the later they occur in the project.
- Large projects can take long periods of time before a usable project is produced—during this time, requirements can change.

This exercise should be marked according to the generic ITGS extended response rubric for SL and HL Paper 1. This can be found in the ITGS Specimen Papers.

Exercise 15-8
a)
i)
Technical document is documentation for developers who maintain or change the system, not end-users. [1 mark] It documents how the system works, its design, and its data structures. [1 mark]

ii)
Phased changeover—this is when part of the organisation starts to use the new system while the rest continues to use the old system.

Parallel changeover—this is when the new system is introduced and used alongside the old system (simultaneously).

Award 1 mark for the method identified and 1 mark for a description, up to 4 marks.

Do not allow: a direct changeover—the company is clearly a large one and such a direct changeover could be considered risky.

b)
Possible answers include:
- Determining an accurate requirements specification to avoid costly changes in the project at a later date—this is difficult unless client-developer communication is very good.
- Selecting a development team who are capable and can deliver on time—it is difficult to assess a developer's background and experience.
- Meeting the project's time and budget goals—this requires very careful planning based on a good understanding of the project requirements and experience of project development.

Grade according to the 6 mark Explanation rubric on page 141.

c)
Possible answers include:
Benefits of a legacy system
- Staff know the current system—no re-training or development of new resources will be required.
- The legacy system may meet the organisation's needs perfectly well.

Drawbacks of a legacy system
- The system may lack potential to be expanded to add new features or meet new requirements.
- Legacy hardware may be needed just to run the system (expensive to maintain).
- The system may be incompatible with other newer systems in the organisation.
- Staff workflow may be limited by the system / they may use inefficient approaches or procedures that are required by the legacy system.

Benefits of developing a new system
- New business requirements could be incorporated into the new system.
- Workflow can be optimised

Drawbacks of developing a new system
- There may be little worth in developing a new system that performs exactly the same job as the old system.
- Systems can be very expensive to develop
- Systems can take a great deal of time to develop
- Many IT projects fail
- Staff re-training will be required (an added expense).

This exercise should be marked according to the generic ITGS extended response rubric for SL and HL Paper 1. This can be found in the ITGS Specimen Papers.

Exercise 15-9

a)

i)

A legacy system is an IT system that is no longer supported by its supplier or developer [1 mark] but which still functions correctly [1 mark].

ii)

The client is an individual or organisation who commissions / initiates the project development process [1 mark] whereas the end user is an individual or group of people who will use the system when it is finished [1 mark].

The client works with the developers to specify the project's overall goals and requirements [1 mark] whereas the end users may work with the developers to explain more detailed aspects of individual processes [1 mark].

b)

Possible answers include:

- Face to face training—people who are experienced with the new system could hold classes or lectures where they demonstrate the new system and explain how to use it.
- Instruction manuals—users could learn the system using instruction manuals, following exercises in them at their own pace.
- Online training—classes could be set up using a Virtual Learning Environment, where resources and tasks are made available on line.
- Tutorials—A series of tutorials (video or text, online or offline) could be created—these could help users perform common tasks associated with the new system.

Grade according to the 6 mark Explanation rubric on page 141.

c)

Possible answers include:

Benefits of commercial off-the-shelf software

- The price is likely to be lower.
- A vast amount of knowledge and help is likely to be available—for example, from the supplier, online, in book stores.
- Major bugs in the software are likely to have already been found and fixed.

Drawbacks of commercial off-the-shelf software

- The software may include many features that are not required.
- The software may not include some features that are required.

- It is not usually possible to expand / customize the software to meet an organisation's individual needs.
- An individual or organisation has little say in the direction the software will be developed in the future (e.g. which new features are added).
- Users may have to alter their work flow to accommodate the software.

Benefits of a custom / bespoke application

- The software can be customised to include precisely the features the organisation requires.
- The software can be changed later to meet new requirements.
- A major competitive advantage can be gained over rivals who do not have the software.

Drawbacks of a custom bespoke application

- Finding a competent developer is a difficult process.
- Developing an IT project is a risky process—and many projects fail.
- A great deal of time needs to be spent on the development process.
- Major bugs may still exist in the software.
- If the developer goes bust, the organisation may be "stranded" without help, support, or a means to further develop the software (bespoke developers tend to be small compared to the biggest commercial software vendors).

This exercise should be marked according to the generic ITGS extended response rubric for SL and HL Paper 1. This can be found in the ITGS Specimen Papers.

Chapter 16
AI & Robotics

Chapter 16 Solutions

Exercise 16-1

The aim of this exercise for students to think about the different types of intelligence which might exist: from mathematical and logical intelligence to creative intelligence. (This can be linked to TOK's *Ways of Knowing*)

Exercise 16-2

The aim of this exercise is to get students to think about acts that are considered "intelligent". Students should be encouraged to think about specific examples rather than give general answers such as "remember things". In many cases there will be computer equivalents of the examples students give ("remember things" is similar to "store data"). These can be used to further drive discussion. (This can be linked to TOK's *Ways of Knowing*)

Exercise 16-3

This exercise has caused some controversy in my classroom at times! Some students attempt to take the easy way out and say "a computer could never be intelligent". A good response to this is "What if you didn't know it was a computer?". This of course is moving students towards thinking about something similar to the Turing Test.

Students should be encouraged to give specific answers – for example, rather than saying "the computer should be able to pass a test", students should give specific examples of the types of questions computers must be able to answer to be considered "intelligent". This is harder than it seems!

Exercise 16-4

The aim of this exercise is to get students thinking about the nature of knowledge. There is clearly no one right answer in this exercise.

Searle famously argued that neither the individual components nor the "mechanism" as a whole "knew" Chinese. He used the Chinese Room to argue that computers only ever manipulated symbols with no understanding of their meaning, and thus would never be able to "understand".

Some of Searle's opponents argued that while none of the individual components of the "system" "know" Chinese, at some point the combination of the books, the man, and the room created understanding of the language. Of course, a lot of these arguments also rest on what we mean by "know" and "understand". (There are strong links to TOK here)

Exercise 16-5

There is a large range of possible knowledge domains students can select. Ideas might include expert systems that:

- Recommend restaurants
- Recommend universities or IB courses
- Recommend pet
- Recommend sports equipment (e.g. type of surf board)
- Diagnose computer faults

Problems students might encounter during the construction of the rules include:

- Some conditions are not absolute, but are 'more true' or 'less true' (fuzzy).
- Some questions may need to be repeated for multiple branches.

Exercise 16-6

This is a practical exercise to familiarise students with various expert systems.

Exercise 16-7

Possible answers include:

- Rule-based intelligence seem intelligent, but may fail to act 'intelligently' at critical moments, because it lacks rules for a given situation.
- Rule-based artificial intelligence has severe limitations in terms of achieving human-like intelligence.
- Striving for computational intelligence may lead to the development of machines that learn for themselves—this may have positive and negative impacts.
- There are great ethical issues related to developing machines which think and learn as humans do.
- Striving for computational intelligence may lead to a greater understanding of our own intelligence.
- The tasks that are hardest for machines are those for which there are no fixed set of rules—therefore, the development of computational intelligence may provide greater benefits.

This exercise should be marked according to the generic ITGS extended response rubric for SL and HL Paper 1. This can be found in the ITGS Specimen Papers.

Exercise 16-8

Possible answers include:

- Bipedal robots are hard to create – the processing and software requirements to simply stand upright on two feet are extremely high. Moving around a room while maintaining balance is even more challenging.
- The bipedal form is often not the optimal shape for the task at hand. For example, cleaning robots and rescue robots might need to be small in stature to fit into small spaces and to avoid being knocked over.
- Humans are adaptable – we can perform many tasks (such as picking up different tools). Many robots are specialised to a single task domain and therefore it makes little sense to make them so adaptable. For example, it makes more sense to fix a robot with tools permanently than to give it human-like arms and hands to grasp a variety of tools.

Exercise 16-9

a)

Possible answers include:

- Ultrasonic sensors which can detect obstacles
- "Cliff sensors", which are simply ultrasonic sensors pointing downwards (if the distance becomes more than a few centimetres, the robot is hanging over an edge).
- Touch sensors to let the robot detect that it has collided with an object
- Internal maps of a room built up using data from the sensors
- GPS systems to help the robot return to previous locations

Grade according to the 6 mark Explanation rubric on page 141.

b)

Possible answers include:

- The robots maintain an internal map of the room, built up using data from their sensors.
- Their software ensures that the robot makes at least one pass over each area of the room.
- "Dirt sensors" (which detect vibration caused by dirt particles) can help the robot determine which areas are dirtier than others.

Grade according to the 6 mark Explanation rubric on page 141.

Exercise 16-10

Grade according to the rubric on page 139.

Exercise 16-11

a)

Possible answers include:

- Obstacle avoidance – the vehicle must avoid a wide range of potential objects including rocks in the road, holes in the road, livestock, people, cliffs, and obstacles that the designers may not have considered.
- Distinguishing the road from other terrain – the vehicle must be able to determine which part of the desert represents the road and which does not. This typically requires a method of detecting the road edge.
- Determining safe driving speeds for a given road section – safe speeds may vary depending on weather conditions, surface type, and incline – and the vehicle must be able to determine this for itself.
- Avoiding other vehicles – and determining a safe place to overtake.
- Navigational issues – finding the correct route.
- Dealing with vehicle problems – including issues that may require it to stop (such as overheating, or a punctured tyre).

Award 1 mark for the method identified and 1 mark for a description, up to 6 marks.

b)

Possible answers include:

- Road obstacles can be detected using a variety of sensors, including ultrasonic sensors and lasers. The sensors should be placed at different positions and heights around the vehicle to detect obstacles at different relative positions (for example, those in its direct path, those near the edge of the road, those in the distance).
- Lasers can be used to detect the road, by looking for smooth areas of terrain that represent the driving surface, and rough terrain which marks the edge of the road and beyond.
- Video cameras and image analysis software can also be used to detect the road. Software can look for areas of different colour which may represent the tarmac of the road compared to the sandy desert.
- Navigation can be achieved using GPS signals. Vehicles can move towards the next GPS "waypoint", but use the technologies above to determine the precise route there.
- Vehicular problems can be detected relatively easily

using sensors – for example, temperature sensors to detect engine problems or pressure sensors to detect tyre problems.

Grade according to the 6 mark Explanation rubric on page 141.

Exercise 16-12

Highlander and Sandstorm

- Highlander / Sandstorm are programmed with GPS coordinates of the route.
- A speed is programmed for each section of the track.
- This means the route must be meticulously prepared.
- This approach is one of *artificial intelligence*: the system mimics the behaviour of a human (driving), but the method it uses is not human-like.

Grade according to the 4 mark Explanation rubric on page 140.

Stanley

- Stanley analyses the road ahead using a video camera, colour recognition, and other factors to assess the road conditions.
- It uses these factors to determine its own safe driving speed.
- When a human is driving the car, Stanley's software is monitoring the driving techniques used and learning from them.
- This behaviour demonstrates *computational intelligence*: the creation of intelligence that operates in a manner similar to humans, and learns.

Grade according to the 4 mark Explanation rubric on page 140.

Exercise 16-13

This activity is designed to link to TOK, in particular "The Arts" Area of Knowledge and the "Emotion" Way of Knowing. Students should consider factors including:

- Does the intention of the artist influence whether something counts as art?
- Does the emotional response of the audience influence whether something counts as art?
- Can we judge something as art (or not art) if we do not know its origin or creator?

Exercise 16-14

a)

Possible answers include:

- Avoiding collisions with people – this is a problem because the person (who is already fragile) could be seriously injured if they were hit by a robot.
- Picking up injured soldiers would be difficult – injured people must be handled in a particular way depending on the injury, and the robot could conceivably exacerbate the injury.

Award 1 mark for the challenge identified and 1 mark for a description, up to 4 marks.

b)

Possible answers include:

Avoiding collisions with people

- A range of sensors to detect nearby objects could be used—the robot could be programmed to slow down or change direction if it is close to an obstacle.
- Touch sensors could be used on the side of the robot—it could stop moving or reverse if one of the sensors was activated.

Picking up injured soldiers

- A computer vision system (for example, a video camera and pattern recognition software) could be used to identify the soldier and their orientation.
- The robot could use this information to slide its arms or a stretcher under the soldier.
- The function of picking up the injured soldier could be remotely controlled by a human—this might allow for greater accuracy.

Grade according to the 6 mark Explanation rubric on page 141.

Exercise 16-15

Possible answers include:

- Robots may be viewed as more acceptable in everyday applications if they look less out of place.
- A negative side effect of this may be increased use of robots in the home and social settings—this may increase the social isolation of some people (for example, elderly people being cared for by robots).
- Robots that look quite similar to humans but not identical are likely to be more disconcerting than robots that are clearly non-human (the 'uncanny valley').
- Some people may feel uncomfortable being surrounded by machines that they are unable to distinguish from people.

- Androids may look like humans but not behave like them—this could lead to a number of impacts, including injuries to people who did not realise they were working near a robot.
- There may be privacy or intellectual property issues if manufacturers attempt to make androids in the likeness of celebrities or other famous people.

This exercise should be marked according to the generic ITGS extended response rubric for SL and HL Paper 1. This can be found in the ITGS Specimen Papers.

Exercise 16-16
Possible answers include:
- The development of certain robots (for example manufacturing robots or cleaning robots) may cause people to lose their jobs—these people also tend to be poorer people in lower paid jobs, who may find it hard to find another job.
- Military robots may be considered unethical if they are used to kill people in a 'more efficient' way—the use of robots may encourage the waging of war since fewer losses will be suffered.
- It could be argued that spending money on these developments in inappropriate; that the money could be better spent elsewhere.
- Some of the jobs taken over by robots are monotonous or dangerous jobs—robots improve safety.
- Some jobs taken by robots will be replaced by new jobs, such as maintaining or repairing the robots. However, these jobs may require more education or qualifications than the jobs they replace.

This exercise should be marked according to the generic ITGS extended response rubric for SL and HL Paper 1. This can be found in the ITGS Specimen Papers.

Exercise 16-17
a)
i)
Natural language processing describes the techniques used to make a computer process human languages [1 mark] as input or output. [1 mark]

ii)
- User interface—prompts the user with questions and allows the input of answers.
- Inference engine—attempts to generate answers from the knowledge base, using input from the user interface.

- Knowledge base—contains the rules relating to a specific knowledge domain.

Award 1 mark for the component identified and 1 mark for a description, up to 4 marks.

b)
- There is no need to travel to visit a doctor—this saves time and money.
- Patients may prefer a computer interface if they are asking questions about embarrassing conditions.
- Doctors can benefit from accessing detailed information on topics that may be outside their field of expertise (for example, tropical diseases).
- An online expert system provides access to patients even if they are geographically far away.
- Many users can consult an online expert at once.
- The expert system will provide consistent results, without forgetting or overlooking something.

Grade according to the 6 mark Explanation rubric on page 141.

c)
Possible answers:
Advantages of machine translation
- Can provide a quick translation without the need for a human translator.
- Large amounts of text can be translated more quickly than a human translator.
- Machine translation may be very cheap or free—human translators typically charge high prices.

Concerns about machine translation
- Translations may be low-quality, which can appear unprofessional if used in some contexts (such as business).
- Machine translations may have problems with context, where words can have multiple or ambiguous meanings depending on their use.
- A machine translation may not capture the tone of a text (such as sarcasm).
- Machine translation may struggle with idioms, where literal translation makes no sense (e.g., 'the apple of my eye' or 'the early bird gets the worm'.
- Machine translation can struggle with slang.
- Machine translation may not function correctly if the source document contains spelling mistakes, grammatical errors, or abbreviations.

This exercise should be marked according to the generic ITGS extended response rubric for SL and HL Paper 1. This can be found in the ITGS Specimen Papers.

Exercise 16-18

a)

i)

A robot is a computer controller device [1 mark] that performs manual, physical tasks. [1 mark]

ii)

Possible answers include:

Input devices

- Hand controls / paddles
- Switches (on hand controls)
- Pressure sensor (on headrest)

Output devices

- Robotic arms
- Robotic grippers / claws
- Screens

b)

Possible answers include:

- Patient support robots / companion robots—these can be used to support patients who have difficulty walking. They can also provide reminders about medicine routines.
- Guide robots—these can help visitors find requested parts of a hospital.
- Transport robots—these can be used to transport hospital supplies (such as meal carts or laundry) around the hospital without human intervention.

Grade according to the 6 mark Explanation rubric on page 141.

c)

Possible answers include:

Benefits

- Patients can get access to the medical care even if their local doctors have limited experience of the procedure.
- Patients can be operated on at their local hospital rather than having to travel many miles to find a capable surgeon.
- Doctors could operate on people in locations that lack medical care—such as on board a ship or in space.

Concerns

- Reliability and speed of network connection—the bandwidth must be sufficiently high and the latency sufficiently low to enable real time communication between the remote doctor and the robotic surgery system. Any lag in feedback could result in surgical errors being made.

- The kind of dedicated, high speed networks required by such systems are extremely expensive.
- Failover / standby systems such as backup power are needed in both locations—this is to prevent harm to the patient if there is an equipment failure at either location.
- Standby staff are needed in the surgery room—they are essential to assist the remote doctor and to take care of any potential problems that cannot be fixed by the robotic surgery system.
- The network must be secure from interference and unauthorised access—in the worst case scenarios, unauthorised access to the network connection could result in disabling or even controlling the connection between doctor and patient.
- Patients may be reluctant to use the system—they may fear equipment or network failure, or "out of control robots". These concerns must be solved before the system can be widely implemented.

This exercise should be marked according to the generic ITGS extended response rubric for SL and HL Paper 1. This can be found in the ITGS Specimen Papers.

Exercise 16-19

a)

i)

Haptic feedback uses feeling or touch (such as vibrations) [1 mark] to provide feedback to the user of a computer system, increasing immersion. [1 mark]

ii)

Possible answers include:

- Lasers—these are used to measure distance by measuring light reflected from surfaces.
- Ultra sonic sensors—these are used to measure distance by using sound reflected from surfaces.
- Touch sensors—these are used to detect a collision with another object.
- Video camera and image recognition software—the software can use pattern recognition to 'search' the video image for distinguishing characteristics (such as the grey of the road).

Award 1 mark for the method identified and 1 mark for a description, up to 4 marks.

Do not allow 'video camera' without an indication that software processes the video feed.

b)

Possible answers include:

- Care must be taken to ensure rescue robots do not accidentally injure victims—for example, picking them up inappropriately or colliding with them.
- Care must be taken to ensure robots do not accidentally reveal the location of friendly troops.
- Care must be taken to ensure controllers of combat robots correctly identify targets before firing weapons—this is necessary to avoid injury to civilians or friendly forces.
- There are many potential problems related to human-robot collisions, which could seriously injure soldiers.
- There may be concern about the future development of such robots, and whether they will be given the power to make decisions autonomously.

Grade according to the 6 mark Explanation rubric on page 141.

c)

Benefits of developing robotic technology
- Robots can perform tasks that are impossible for humans—such as the exploration of alien planets. This helps increase our scientific understanding.
- Robots can perform tasks that are dangerous for humans—such as fighting fires or cleaning up nuclear accidents. This puts fewer humans in danger.
- Robots often perform monotonous tasks such as factory jobs—which they can perform more efficiently and for longer than humans.

Concerns about developing robotic technology
- Many robotic developments (such as factory robots) cause people to lose their jobs. This can lead to related issues, including economic and social problems.
- Some robotic developments may be considered unethical by some (for example, the development of military drones) - but these can go ahead because legal frameworks take time to catch up with technology.
- There may be negative health effects associated with a less active lifestyle if robots perform an increasing number of our tasks—for example, cleaning and other domestic helper robots.

This exercise should be marked according to the generic ITGS extended response rubric for SL and HL Paper 1. This can be found in the ITGS Specimen Papers.

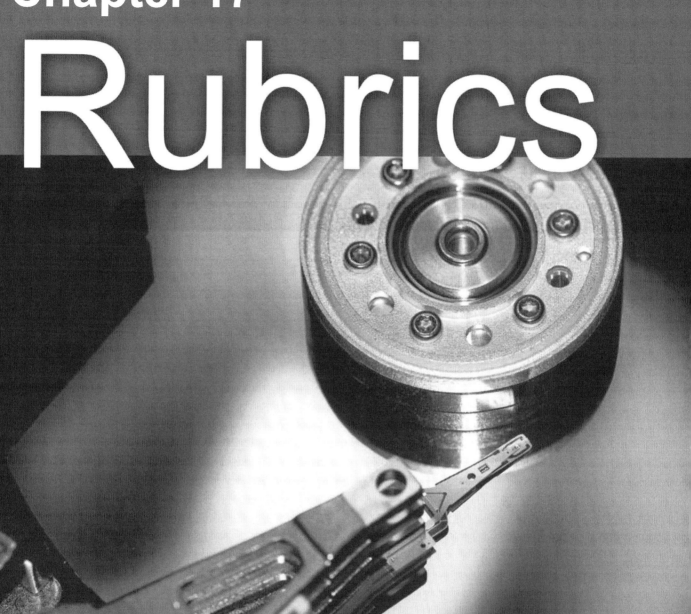

Chapter 17
Rubrics

Chapter 17—Assessment Rubrics

Exercise 1-4

Student name:

Marks	Level Descriptor
1-2 marks	A limited understanding of the ITGS issues and impacts. Limited reference to the affected stakeholders. Little or no correct reference to the appropriate areas of application. Little or no correct use of IT terminology.
3-4 marks	Some understanding of the ITGS issues and impacts, though mostly descriptive. There is correct reference to some stakeholders. The correct areas of application are described. There is some correct use of IT terminology.
5-6 marks	Detailed and clear understanding. The ITGS issues and impacts are fully explained with clear reasoning. The correct stakeholders are all described. The correct areas of application are described. IT terminology is always correctly used and is linked explicitly to the ITGS issues and impacts it causes.

Grade: / 6

Comments:

Exercise 1-5

Student name:

	Level Descriptors			
Item	1 mark	2 marks	3 marks	4 marks
Use of appropriate sources	Few sources are relevant to the ITGS course content. A limited range of sources is used, some of questionable reliability, or citations have significant omissions.	Some sources are relevant to the ITGS course content. A limited range of sources is used, or some sources are of questionable reliability. Most sources are cited.	Most sources are relevant to the ITGS course content. A wide range of sources are used. Most are reliable, and most are cited correctly.	All sources are highly relevant to the ITGS course content. A wide range of reliable sources are used. All sources are correctly cited.
Application of ITGS Triangle	Few strands of the ITGS triangle are covered. The ITGS social / ethical issues are rarely applied correctly.	Each strand of the ITGS triangle is partially covered. The ITGS social / ethical issues are sometimes applied correctly, but with some inconsistency or errors.	Each strand of the ITGS triangle is well covered. The ITGS social / ethical issues are usually applied correctly and consistently.	Each strand of the ITGS triangle is thoroughly covered. The ITGS social / ethical issues are applied correctly and consistently.
Presentation	Good presentation, with a few minor errors. The characteristics of the medium have generally been well used.	Well presented, with no errors such as typing mistakes. Excellent use has been made of the medium's characteristics to create an interesting and detailed presentation.		

Grade: / 10

Comments:

Exercise 2-7

Student name:

Marks	Level Descriptor
1 mark	The chosen computer does not fit the scenario requirements. There may be some relevant aspects of the computer's specification identified. There is no justification of the choice of computer.
2 marks	The chosen computer fits the scenario requirements well. Most relevant aspects of the computer's specification is identified. There is a limited justification of the choice of computer, with limited reference to the specification or the scenario.
3 marks	The chosen computer fits the scenario requirements well. Most relevant aspects of the computer's specification is identified. There is a clear and correct justification for the choice of computer, which usually references the computer's specification and the scenario.
4 marks	The chosen computer fits the scenario requirements well. Each relevant aspect of the computer's specification is identified. There is a clear and correct justification for the choice of computer, which clearly references the computer's specification and the scenario.

Scenario (a) grade: / 4
Scenario (b) grade: / 4
Scenario (c) grade: / 4

Comments:

Exercise 3-1

Student name:

Item	Level Descriptors			
	1 mark	**2 marks**	**3 marks**	**4 marks**
Answer, Analysis, and Evaluation (/ 4)	Very basic, brief statements Very little knowledge or understanding Almost entirely common sense and/or general knowledge Little or no reference to the specific situation. Significant errors or omissions.	Limited and descriptive answer with common sense and/or general knowledge. Some supporting evidence. Reference to the specific situation in parts.	Detailed, mostly balanced answer making clear reference to specific examples. Clear conclusions, with good evidence to support them. Good ability to reason and judge Good consideration of the specific situation in most of the answer.	Detailed and balanced answer making clear reference to specific examples. Clear conclusions, with excellent and balanced evidence. Excellent ability to reason and judge Excellent consideration of the specific situation throughout.
Use of technical language (/ 4)	Basic use of technical language, but with significant errors or omissions.	Some correct use of technical language, but some important errors or omissions.	Thorough, generally correct, and relevant use of technical language. Only minor omissions or errors.	Thorough, complete, correct, and relevant use of technical language throughout.
Presentation technique (/ 2)	Some good presentation techniques are demonstrated.	Consistent use of most 'good presentation' techniques		

Grade: / 10

Comments:

Exercise 3-2

Student name:

Item	Level Descriptors			
	1 mark	**2 marks**	**3 marks**	**4 marks**
Answer, Analysis, and Evaluation (/ 4)	Very basic, brief statements Very little knowledge or understanding Almost entirely common sense and/or general knowledge Little or no reference to the Therac-25 case study. Significant errors or omissions.	Limited and descriptive answer with common sense and/or general knowledge. Some supporting evidence. Some reference to the Therac-25 case study.	Detailed answer making clear reference to specific examples. Clear conclusions, with good evidence to support them. Good consideration of the Therac-25 case study in most of the answer.	Detailed answer making clear reference to specific examples. Clear conclusions, with excellent and balanced evidence. Excellent consideration of the Therac-25 case study throughout.
Use of technical language (/ 4)	Basic use of technical language, but with significant errors or omissions.	Some correct use of technical language, but some important errors or omissions.	Thorough, generally correct and relevant use of technical language. Only minor omissions or errors.	Thorough, complete, correct and relevant use of technical language throughout.
Presentation technique & participation (/ 2)	Generally good participation in both asking and addressing questions.	Excellent participation in both asking and addressing questions.		

Grade: / 10

Comments:

Exercise 3-4
Student name:

Marks	Level Descriptor
1 mark	The failure is identified or briefly described. There is a very brief description of the impacts of the failure and its causes. Use of appropriate IT and ITGS language is rare.
2-3 marks	The failure is described using some appropriate IT terminology. The impacts of the failure are described, though not always using ITGS language. The causes of the failure are described, though not always using ITGS language.
4 marks	The failure is clearly and accurately described using appropriate IT terminology. The impacts of the failure are clearly described using ITGS language. The causes of the failure are clearly identified and described using ITGS language.

Scenario (1) grade: / 4
Scenario (2) grade: / 4
Scenario (3) grade: / 4

Comments:

Exercise 5-9

Student name:

Item	Level Descriptors				
	1 mark	2 marks	3 marks	4 marks	5 marks
Security risks explanations (/ 5)	Very few or no explanations of security risks, or significant errors.	Some definitions of terms but limited explanation of their effect on the user.	Sufficient explanation of security risks that users face using some ITGS terminology.	Good explanation of security risks using ITGS terminology. Only minor mistakes.	Excellent use of well researched, correct explanations of security risks using ITGS terminology throughout.
Practical Solutions (/ 5)	Very few or no solutions.	Some brief solutions mentioned. No practical advice given.	Sufficient solutions and practical advice.	Good, practical solutions, clearly explained.	Excellent use of correct, clear, practical solutions with supporting material (e.g. hyperlinks to recommended software)
Design, Layout & Technical Skills (/ 5)	Poor design & layout skills, the use of a template, or the use of images without citation.	Some design techniques applied to layout, images, fonts, or text. Sources are cited (though perhaps incorrectly)	Sufficient design skills including layout, images, and text. Sources are cited (generally correctly)	Good design skills including appropriate use of layout, use of images, fonts, and text. Correct citations for all material.	Excellent design skills including layout, use of images, fonts, and text. Correct citations for all material.

Grade: / 15

Comments:

Exercise 6-2

Student name:

Item	Level Descriptors			
	1 mark	2 marks	3 marks	4 marks
Description of changes (/ 4)	Changes are identified. Very little understanding of the topic is demonstrated.	Some changes are identified using correct technical language.	All changes are described. Technical language is generally used accurately.	All changes are clearly described using technical language accurately throughout.
Explanation of impacts (/ 4)	Several impacts are identified but not described. Use of ITGS terminology is very limited. Significant errors or omissions.	Several impacts are described but not explained. There is some use of ITGS terminology. Some errors or omissions.	Impacts are explained in a balanced way. Correct ITGS terminology is used frequently. Only minor errors or omissions.	Impacts are clearly explained in a balanced way. ITGS terminology is used correctly throughout. No errors or omissions.

Image 1 grade: / 8
Image 2 grade: / 8

Comments:

Exercise 6-15

Student name:

Item	Level Descriptors				
	1 mark	**2 marks**	**3 marks**	**4 marks**	**5 marks**
Use of ITGS language (/5)	Very limited use of technical language. Many mistakes or omissions.	Occasional correct use of technical language. Several mistakes or omissions	Some correct use of technical language. Only minor mistakes or omissions.	Mostly complete and correct use of technical language. Only minor mistakes. No omissions.	Complete and correct use of technical language throughout. No mistakes or omissions.
Decisions & ethical considerations (/5)	A limited number of decisions described, with little or no justification. There is little or no reference to impacts and stakeholders. No supporting examples. A very small range of digital manipulations is covered. Significant mistakes or omissions.	An attempt to justify some decisions, with limited reference to impacts and stakeholders. Limited supporting examples. Some appropriate types of digital manipulation are covered. Some mistakes or omissions.	Some decisions are explained or justified. There is some reference to impacts and stakeholders. Some decisions are supported by appropriate examples. Most appropriate types of digital manipulation are covered. Only minor mistakes or omissions	Most decision are explained and justified, usually with clear reference to impacts and stakeholders. Most decisions are supported by clear and appropriate examples. Most appropriate types of digital manipulation are covered. Only minor mistakes. No omissions.	Comprehensive decisions, explained and fully justified, with clear reference to impacts and stakeholders. All decisions are supported by clear and appropriate examples. All appropriate types of digital manipulations are covered. No mistakes or omissions.

Grade: / 15

Comments:

Exercise 6-17

Student name:

| Item | Level Descriptors | | | | |
	1 mark	2 marks	3 marks	4 marks	5 marks
Presentation design & presentation skills (/5)	Few elements of good presentation design are used. Few elements of good presentation technique are used. There may be large lapses or omissions.	Some elements of good presentation design are used. Some elements of good presentation technique are used. There are many minor lapses or one or two major lapses.	Several elements of good presentation design are used. Some elements of good presentation technique are used. There are some minor lapses in one or both areas.	The presentation design and the presenters' skills are very good: all points are thoroughly covered with only minor lapses.	Both the presenters' skills and the presentation design are excellent, demonstrating a clear knowledge and understanding of appropriate techniques.
Explanation of topic (/5)	A very basic answer which demonstrates little understanding. Very little or no use of ITGS language.	A limited answer, with some description and some explanations and reasons. Some correct use of ITGS language.	An adequate response, with some description and some explanations and reasons. Generally correct use of ITGS language.	Some understanding is demonstrated, but parts may be unclear or inconsistent. Consistent correct use of ITGS language.	A detailed response which includes clear and detailed explanation and reasons. Consistent, detailed, and correct use of ITGS language.

Grade: / 10

Comments:

Exercise 7-10
Student name:

Item	Level Descriptors			
	1 mark	2 marks	3 marks	4 marks
Database setup (/4)	Significant amounts of redundant data, with many incorrect or missing relationships. Use of primary keys and appropriate data types is poor and shows a lack of understanding of the topic.	Normalisation has been attempted but some redundant data remains. Several tables lack primary keys or have incorrect primary keys. Several fields have inappropriate data types. Some relationships are missing or contain errors.	Tables are fully normalised and correct relationships have been added. Most tables have correct primary keys, and most fields are present and use the correct data types. No significant omissions.	Tables are fully normalised and correct relationships have been added. All tables have correct primary keys and all required fields are present and use the appropriate data types.
Validation & verification (/4)	A limited range of validation techniques has been used. There are many significant omissions.	Some validation techniques have been used, but there are some important omissions.	A full range of validation techniques has been used, usually appropriately.	A full range of validation techniques has been used, always appropriately.
Queries (/4)	A limited number of basic queries have been created, and lack functionality.	Most appropriate queries have been created. Not all queries work as required.	All appropriate queries have been created and almost all are fully functional.	All appropriate queries have been created and are fully functional.
Forms and Reports (/4)	At least one form and one report have been created.	Several required forms and reports have been created, but with the use of wizards, and minimal customization.	Most required forms and reports have been created. There is some evidence of customization and/or use of advanced queries.	All required forms and reports have been created, and customized to provide appropriate and relevant appearance and layout.

Grade: / 16

Comments:

Exercise 7-15
Student name:

Marks	Level Descriptor
1-2 marks	A limited range of new tables and fields has been added. The database contains a significant amount of redundant data. There are few correct relationships indicated.
3-4 marks	Several new tables are included in the diagram. Some relevant fields have been added. Most relationships have been added and are correct, with only some errors or omissions. The data is mostly normalised, with some errors or omissions.
5-6 marks	Multiple new tables are included in the diagram. An appropriate range of relevant fields have been added. All relationships are correct and none are missing. The data is fully normalised.

Grade: / 6

Comments:

Exercise 7-15 Sample diagram

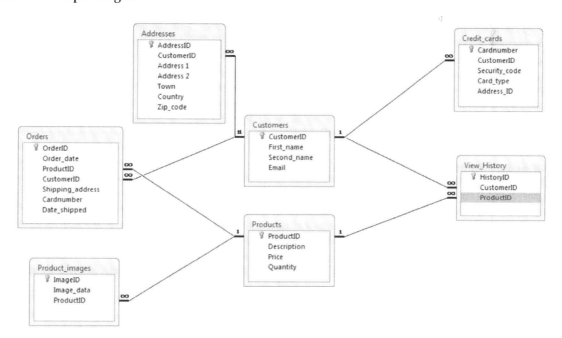

Exercise 9-1

Student name:

Item	Level Descriptors				
	1 mark	2 marks	3 marks	4 marks	5 marks
Explanation of monitoring techniques (/5)	A very limited range of monitoring techniques are covered (fewer than 4).	Some monitoring techniques are covered (fewer than 5).	A satisfactory number of monitoring techniques are covered, including those that will be used and those that won't.	A good range of monitoring techniques are covered, including those that will be used and those that won't.	The policy covers all common monitoring techniques; those that will be used and those that won't.
	Techniques are sometimes explained but with little or no technical language.	Techniques are sometimes explained but with limited technical language.	Most techniques are correctly explained with some technical language.	Techniques are generally clearly and correctly explained with technical language.	The techniques are clearly and correctly explained with technical language.
Justification of policy (/5)	Little or no attempt to justify the techniques.	A justification is attempted for some items but may lack detail.	There is a clear and balanced justification of each item, addressing the social impacts.	There is a clear, detailed, and balanced justification of most items, addressing the impacts and ethical issues.	There is a clear, detailed, and balanced justification of each item, addressing the impacts and ethical issues.
	Little or no reference to social impacts.	Reference to social impacts is scarce.			

Grade: / 10

Comments:

Exercise 9-10
Student name:

Marks	Level Descriptor
1-2 marks	Some pages are included, but there are significant omissions. Pages are not ordered logically — there may be too many or too few sub-groupings. The hierarchy is unbalanced (either too wide or too deep).
3-4 marks	Most pages are included. Pages are ordered into logical groups. The hierarchy is generally balanced (the number of links on each page is generally neither too small nor too great).
5-6 marks	All required pages are included. Pages are ordered into logical groups. The hierarchy is balanced (the number of links on each page is neither too small nor too great).

Grade: / 6

Comments:

Exercise 9-10 Sample diagram
(Only a subset of the possible pages is shown here)

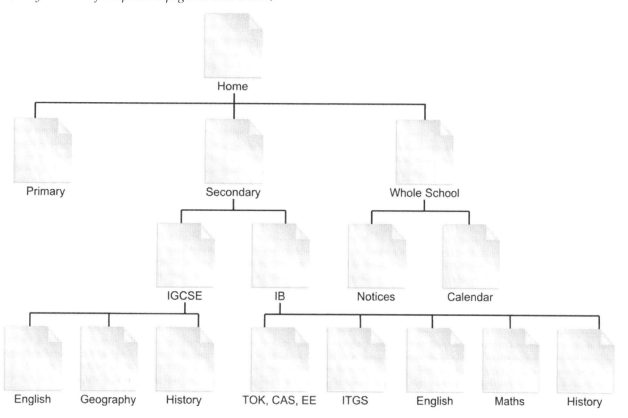

Exercise 9-22

Student name:

Item	Level Descriptors			
	1 mark	2 marks	3 marks	4 marks
Site design & Site map **(/ 2)**	Pages are sometimes organized in a clear and logical manner. The sitemap diagram is of an acceptable standard and could be followed to create the web site.	Pages are organized in a clear and logical manner. The sitemap diagram is of a high standard and could be easily followed to create the web site.		
Good web design guidelines **(/ 4)**	Design is based upon templates Page design is not appropriate for the task. Page design is largely inconsistent Each page is well laid out Navigation options are clear	Design is based on modified templates Page design is sometimes appropriate for the task. Page design is consistent across some pages Each page is well laid out Navigation options are clear	Design is original (no templates) Page design is appropriate for the task. Page design is generally consistent across most pages Most pages are well laid out Navigation options are clear	Design is original (no templates) Page design is highly appropriate for the task. Page design is consistent across the web site Each page is well laid out Navigation options are clear
Content skills **(/ 4)**	Content is rarely appropriate for the chosen scenario No appropriate multimedia elements have been included Few or no appropriate SEO **or** accessibility techniques have been used	Content is sometimes appropriate for the chosen scenario Few appropriate multimedia elements have been included Some appropriate SEO **or** accessibility techniques have been used	Content is appropriate for the chosen scenario Some appropriate multimedia elements have been included Some appropriate SEO **and** accessibility techniques have been used	Content is highly appropriate for the chosen scenario A range of appropriate multimedia elements have been included Appropriate SEO **and** accessibility techniques have been used throughout

Grade: / 10

Comments:

Exercise 10-6

Student name:

Item	Level Descriptors			
	1-2 marks	**3-4 marks**	**5-6 marks**	**7-8 marks**
Presentation **(/ 4)**	Good presentation, with a few minor errors. The characteristics of the medium have generally been well used.	Well presented, with no errors such as typing mistakes. Excellent use has been made of the medium's characteristics to create an interesting presentation.		
Evaluation of educational technology **(/ 8)**	Very basic, brief statements. Very little knowledge or understanding	Limited and descriptive answer with common sense and/or general knowledge.	Detailed, mostly balanced answer making clear reference to specific examples.	Detailed and balanced answer making clear reference to specific examples.
	Almost entirely common sense and/or general knowledge	Some supporting evidence.	Good ability to reason and judge	Excellent ability to reason and judge
	Little or no reference to the specific situation.	Reference to the specific situation in parts.	Good consideration of the specific situation in most of the answer.	Excellent consideration of the specific situation throughout.
	Significant errors or omissions.	A range of appropriate technology is covered, with minor omissions	A wide range of appropriate technology is covered	A wide range of appropriate technology is covered
Future projections **(/ 8)**	No conclusions are made, or conclusions are made without supporting examples, evidence, and arguments.	Conclusions are made about the future impact of technology, sometimes supported by examples, evidence, and arguments.	Conclusions are made about the future impact of technology, usually supported by examples, evidence, and arguments.	Clear conclusions are made about the future impact of technology, always supported by examples, evidence, and arguments.

Grade: / 20

Comments:

Exercise 12-5

Student name:

Marks	Level Descriptor
1-2 marks	A very limited range of appropriate health problems is covered A very limited range of measures is covered, which are often of limited feasibility The measures are rarely explained. There is limited use of technical language There are several major errors / omissions
3-4 marks	A limited range of appropriate health problems is covered A limited range of measures is covered, which are sometimes of limited feasibility The measures are explained using some technical language where appropriate There are several minor errors / omissions or a small number of larger errors / omissions
5-6 marks	A satisfactory range of appropriate health problems is covered A satisfactory range of generally appropriate and feasible measures is covered The measures are clearly explained using some technical language where appropriate There are several minor errors / omissions or a small number of larger errors / omissions
7-8 marks	A good range of appropriate health problems is covered A good range of appropriate and feasible measures is covered The measures are clearly explained using technical language where appropriate There are only minor errors or omissions
9-10 marks	A full range of appropriate health problems is covered A full range of appropriate and feasible measures is covered The measures are clearly explained using technical language where appropriate There are no errors or omissions

Grade: / 10

Comments:

Exercise 13-1

Student name:

Item	Level Descriptors			
	1-2 marks	3-4 marks	5-6 marks	7-8 marks
Presentation (/ 4)	Good presentation, with a few minor errors. The characteristics of the medium have generally been well used.	Well presented, with no errors such as spelling mistakes or poor audio quality. Excellent use has been made of the medium's characteristics to create an interesting presentation.		
How smart homes work (/ 8)	Few smart home features have been explained using technical language, or there are significant technical errors.	Some smart home features have been explained using technical language, generally correctly.	Most smart home features have been correctly explained using technical language.	All smart home features have been correctly explained using technical language.
	These explanations have rarely been explicitly linked to the smart home's benefits.	These explanations have sometimes been explicitly linked to the smart home's benefits.	These explanations have been usually explicitly linked to the smart home's benefits.	These explanations have been explicitly linked to the smart home's benefits.
Benefits of smart homes (/ 8)	The benefits have been explained for a limited number of smart home features	The benefits have been explained for some smart home features	The benefits have been clearly explained for most smart home features	The benefits have been clearly and fully explained for each individual feature
	The explanations are clearly supported with evidence and examples	The explanations are supported with some evidence and examples	The explanations are clearly supported with evidence and examples	The explanations are clearly supported with evidence and examples

Grade: / 20

Comments:

Exercise 14-3

Student name:

Marks	Level Descriptor
1-2 marks	A very limited range of election campaigning technologies is covered Only 'accepted' technologies have been covered There is a basic description of the benefits and drawbacks of each technology There is limited correct use of technical language
3-4 marks	A limited range of election campaigning technologies is covered Only 'accepted' technologies have been covered There are limited references to evidence and examples There is a description of the benefits and drawbacks of each technology There are limited reference to the question There is some correct use of technical language
5-6 marks	A satisfactory range of election campaigning technologies is covered Both 'accepted' and 'rejected' technologies have been covered There are some clear and explicit references to evidence and examples There is an explanation of the benefits and drawbacks of each technology There are some specific references to the question There is a generally balanced analysis, though there may be no conclusion Technical language is used correctly in places
7-8 marks	A good range of election campaigning technologies is covered Both 'accepted' and 'rejected' technologies have been covered There are clear and explicit references to evidence and examples throughout the work There is a clear explanation of the benefits and drawbacks of each technology There is usually specific and clear reference to the question There is a clear and balanced analysis, and a clear conclusion Technical language is usually used correctly
9-10 marks	A full range of election campaigning technologies is covered Both 'accepted' and 'rejected' technologies have been covered There are clear and explicit references to evidence and examples throughout the work There is a clear explanation of the benefits and drawbacks of each technology There is specific and clear reference to the question There is a clear and balanced analysis, and a clear conclusion Technical language is used correctly throughout

Grade: / 10

Comments:

Exercise 16-10

Student name:

Item	Level Descriptors			
	1 mark	2 marks	3 marks	4 marks
Description of task (/ 2)	The tasks performed by the robots are clearly and generally accurately described. There is some correct use of technical language.	The tasks performed by the robots are clearly and accurately described using correct technical language.		
Explanation of social impacts (/ 4)	A limited range robots is covered.	A range of generally appropriate robots is covered.	A range of appropriate robots is covered.	A range of appropriate robots is covered.
	The robots' social impacts are sometimes explained, with limited reference to stakeholders.	The robots' social impacts are described, usually with reference to stakeholders.	The robots' social impacts are clearly and accurately explained, with clear reference to stakeholders.	The robots' social impacts are clearly and accurately explained, with clear reference to stakeholders.
	A limited number of positive and negative impacts are described	Positive and negative impacts are described, though they may be unbalanced.	Positive and negative impacts are explained.	Positive and negative impacts are explained.
Consideration of ethical issues (/ 4)	Few or no appropriate ethical questions are stated.	Appropriate ethical questions are described.	Appropriate ethical questions are examined.	Appropriate and insightful ethical questions are examined.
	No future actions are considered.	Limited future actions are considered.	Some possible future actions are considered.	Possible future actions are considered.

Grade: / 10

Comments:

4 Mark Explanation Rubric

Student name:

Marks	Level Descriptor
1 mark	Very limited understanding of the topic is demonstrated. No reasoning is provided, or there may be significant errors.
2-3 marks	Some understanding is demonstrated. There is some reasoning, although it may be unbalanced, incomplete, or lacking detail.
4 marks	Understanding is clearly demonstrated. The explanation is detailed and shows good awareness of the topic. There are no significant errors.

Grade: / 4

Comments:

4 Mark Explanation Rubric

Student name:

Marks	Level Descriptor
1 mark	Very limited understanding of the topic is demonstrated. No reasoning is provided, or there may be significant errors.
2-3 marks	Some understanding is demonstrated. There is some reasoning, although it may be unbalanced, incomplete, or lacking detail.
4 marks	Understanding is clearly demonstrated. The explanation is detailed and shows good awareness of the topic. There are no significant errors.

Grade: / 4

Comments:

6 Mark Explanation Rubric
Student name:

Marks	Level Descriptor
1-2 marks	Very limited understanding of the topic is demonstrated. No reasoning is provided, or there may be significant errors.
3-4 marks	Some understanding is demonstrated. There is some reasoning, although it may be unbalanced, incomplete, or lacking detail at the lower end of the band.
5-6 marks	Understanding is clearly and fully demonstrated. The explanation shows good awareness of the topic. Reasoning is clear, detailed, and balanced. There are no significant errors.

Grade: / 6

Comments:

6 Mark Explanation Rubric
Student name:

Marks	Level Descriptor
1-2 marks	Very limited understanding of the topic is demonstrated. No reasoning is provided, or there may be significant errors.
3-4 marks	Some understanding is demonstrated. There is some reasoning, although it may be unbalanced, incomplete, or lacking detail at the lower end of the band.
5-6 marks	Understanding is clearly and fully demonstrated. The explanation shows good awareness of the topic. Reasoning is clear, detailed, and balanced. There are no significant errors.

Grade: / 6

Comments:

6 Mark Discuss Rubric
Student name:

Marks	Level Descriptor
1-2 marks	Limited understanding of the topic is demonstrated. Limited reasoning is provided. There is limited use of ITGS terminology. There may be significant errors.
3-4 marks	Some understanding is demonstrated. There is some evaluation, although it may be unbalanced, incomplete, or lacking detail at the lower end of the band. Some ITGS terminology is used, though it may be lacking detail at the lower end of the band.
5-6 marks	Understanding is clearly and fully demonstrated. ITGS terminology is used appropriately throughout. The shows good awareness of the topic. Evaluation is clear, detailed, and balanced.

Grade: / 6

Comments:

6 Mark Discuss Rubric
Student name:

Marks	Level Descriptor
1-2 marks	Limited understanding of the topic is demonstrated. Limited reasoning is provided. There is limited use of ITGS terminology. There may be significant errors.
3-4 marks	Some understanding is demonstrated. There is some evaluation, although it may be unbalanced, incomplete, or lacking detail at the lower end of the band. Some ITGS terminology is used, though it may be lacking detail at the lower end of the band.
5-6 marks	Understanding is clearly and fully demonstrated. ITGS terminology is used appropriately throughout. The shows good awareness of the topic. Evaluation is clear, detailed, and balanced.

Grade: / 6

Comments:

Image Credits

Some images included in this work are distributed under the Creative Commons Attribution (CC-BY) or Creative Commons Share Alike (CC-SA) licences. The text of these licences can be viewed at http://creativecommons.org/licenses/

Some diagrams in this text were constructed using the excellent icons from the Open Clip Art Library (www.openclipart.org), licensed under the Creative Commons Public Domain (CC0) licence.

Unless otherwise noted all images are Copyright © 2010-2013 Stuart Gray

Cover image: miamiamia / SXC / HAAP Media Ltd
Chapter 1 Cover image: nahhan / SXC / HAAP Media Ltd
Chapter 2 Cover image: dreamjay / SXC / HAAP Media Ltd
Chapter 3 Cover image: arinas74 / SXC / HAAP Media Ltd;
Chapter 4 Cover image: pseudoxx / SXC / HAAP Media Ltd
Chapter 5 Cover image: ilco / SXC / HAAP Media Ltd
Chapter 6 Cover image: pooow / SXC / HAAP Media Ltd
Chapter 7 Cover image: mmagallan / SXC / HAAP Media Ltd
Chapter 8 Cover image: Argonne National Laboratory
Chapter 9 Cover image: Speedy2 / SXC / HAAP Media Ltd
Chapter 10 Cover image: Cellanr / CC-SA
Chapter 11 Cover image: Rybson / SXC / HAAP Media Ltd
Chapter 12 Cover image: US Navy / PD
Chapter 13 Cover image: 13-1 Kei Noguchi / CC-SA
Chapter 14: Cover image: US Air Force / PD
Chapter 15 Cover image: mm907ut / SXC / HAAP Media Ltd;
Chapter 16 Cover image: NASA / Public Domain

v1.0

14926961R00086

Printed in Poland
by Amazon Fulfillment
Poland Sp. z o.o., Wrocław